STRATEGY AND PERFORMANCE

Getting the measure of your business

STRATEGY AND PERFORMANCE

Getting the measure of your business

Andy Neely
Michael Bourne
John Mills
Ken Platts
Huw Richards

PUBLISHED BY THE PRESS SYNDICATE OF THE UNIVERSITY OF CAMBRIDGE
The Pitt Building, Trumpington Street, Cambridge, United Kingdom

CAMBRIDGE UNIVERSITY PRESS
The Edinburgh Building, Cambridge CB2 2RU, UK
40 West 20th Street, New York, NY 10011-4211, USA
477 Williamstown Road, Port Melbourne, VIC 3207, Australia
Ruiz de Alarcón 13, 28014 Madrid, Spain
Dock House, The Waterfront, Cape Town 8001, South Africa

http://www.cambridge.org

First published 2002   **Coventry University**

Printed in the United Kingdom at the University Press, Cambridge

Typeface Utopia 9.5/13pt.   *System* QuarkXPress®

A catalogue record for this book is available from the British Library

ISBN 0 521 75031 8 paperback
ISBN 0 521 75032 6 set (with *Getting the Measure of Your Business*
and *Competing through Competences*)

Contents

Section 1

Process overview   9

When embarking on a new venture several questions spring to mind – what is involved, how long will it take, how much resource will it consume, what benefit will there be? These issues are addressed in Section 1.

Section 2

Selecting a facilitator   27

Before launching the process you will need to appoint a process facilitator – someone to manage it. The guide is designed to help you decide who you should appoint as a facilitator.

Section 3

Launching the process   33

Launching the process involves more than simply selecting a facilitator. Identifying, designing and implementing a balanced set of performance measures by its nature requires input from various people. This means that the process, as described here, has to be sold within your organisation. Section 3 contains tools and techniques designed to help you (or your newly appointed facilitator) to launch the process.

Section 4   ## The workbook   37

The how-to guide. It is divided into two phases, each of five
parts. Each individual part is built around a series of practical
worksheets or forms.

Phase 1 (Parts 1 – 5) shows you how to identify, design and
implement a balanced set of top-level measures for your business.

Phase 2 (Parts 6 – 10) explains how these top-level measures
can be cascaded through the organisation so that appropriate
local performance measures are developed.

Acknowledgements

We must first thank those who funded our research for without them we could not have begun. The Engineering and Physical Sciences Research Council provided the first rolling grant in this area of research and Rolls-Royce Aerospace, Leica Lithographic Systems, Ai Qualitek Ltd, Ferodo (now part of Federal Mogul), Berol (now part of Sanford), T&N Technology (now part of Federal Mogul), Domino Printing Sciences, Glacier Vandervell (now part of the Dana Corporation), Rexam, London and Scandinavian Metals, AEM Ltd, James Walker & Co. Ltd, Gilbert Gilkes and Gordon Ltd and Marshall SPV have all provided significant support for the research. The DTI provided funds to support the marketing of the first edition of this workbook.

Many other companies and organisations have supported the research with their valuable time, providing a testing ground for refining and validating our methods. Individuals in these companies have sometimes become researchers themselves, reflecting on our joint experiences and adding their insight to ours, we thank them all.

We also value the encouragement and efforts of academic colleagues, Dr Mark Wilcox (University of Northumbria), Professor David Hamblin (Luton Business School), and Dr John Bicheno (Cardiff Business School) who helped to test this workbook, making its second edition more robust than the first. A special mention must go to Professor Mike Gregory whose interest in converting the theory of manufacturing strategy into tools managers could use lay at the heart of our work.

Introduction

In this introduction we shall answer the following five questions:

1. Why is performance measurement so important?
2. How does performance measurement help me run my business?
3. Is getting the measure going to help me?
4. Why should I take this approach?
5. What should I read next?

1. Why is performance measurement so important?

Performance measurement is on the management agenda:

> To achieve sustainable business success in the demanding world market-place, a company must use relevant performance measures

(UK Government White Paper on Competitiveness).

> World class manufacturing recognises the importance of metrics in helping to define the goals and performance expectation for the organisation. They adopt or develop appropriate metrics to interpret and describe quantitatively the criteria used to measure the effectiveness of the manufacturing system and its many interrelated components.

(one of the ten foundations of world-class practice from the Foundation of Manufacturing Committee of the National Academy of Engineering, USA).

The problem with the performance measures used in many businesses today is that they are financially biased and historically focused. Try listing the five measures that receive most attention in your business:

- Are any of them non-financial?
- Do any of them help you to predict what might be about to happen to your business?
- Or do they simply enable you to review what happened last week, last month, or even last year?

Take, for example, sales turnover. How can you actually use the information this measure provides to manage your business? If sales turnover was £200,000 short of forecast last month, how does measuring sales turnover help you get back on track? How does it help you determine what you should do next?

The answer is it doesn't. In fact, it can't. Sales turnover is undoubtedly a useful indicator, and one that all businesses should review, but it can only ever tell you how you did last week, or last month, or last year. You may use it to motivate your people, but the fundamental problem with it is that it is history. If you want a predictive measure, one that provides an indication of what sales turnover might be at the end of next month, you should be monitoring quotes submitted, or requests received.

Traditionally performance measurement has been seen as a means of monitoring performance, checking progress and identifying areas that need attention.

2. How does performance measurement help me run my business?

One of the greatest problems facing managers today is how to get the strategy implemented. Performance measurement can make a significant contribution to achieving this.

Recent developments suggest that performance measures should be used to:

- Clarify strategy
- Communicate and drive strategy
- Check implementation of strategy
- Challenge strategy

Clarifying strategy

Organisations are complex entities. They consist of varying numbers of people, undertaking different tasks, often in different locations, ideally with the common purpose of delivering value to customers. In theory strategies explain what the organisation will do, what it will not do and why these choices have been made. In practice strategies are often vague, unbounded and incredibly difficult to implement. One of the reasons performance measures have become so popular in recent years is that they provide a means of overcoming these problems.

The process of deciding what to measure and, just as importantly, what not to measure, forces managers to make their priorities and language explicit. No longer is it sufficient to say our strategy is 'to deliver outstanding value to our customers'. Organisations can't measure whether they deliver outstanding value to their customers without defining what is meant by value. It may be that value is perceived value and hence the measure becomes 'do our customers believe that we are delivering value to them?'. It may be that value equates to an ongoing reduction in product lifetime costs, hence the measure would be one that tracked whether or not product lifetime costs were reducing year on year. The point is that by deciding to introduce measures that reflect the organisation's strategies, the precise meaning of the strategies has to be clarified. Once the meaning has been clarified then measurement becomes possible and the strategies themselves become explicit and well bounded. This makes them far easier to implement.

It for this reason that managers are increasingly turning to measurement frameworks like Bob Kaplan and David Norton's balanced scorecard. The balanced scorecard is based on the theory that an organisation's measurement system should enable its managers to answer four fundamental questions:

- How do we look to our shareholders? (the financial perspective)
- How do our customers see us? (the customer perspective)
- What must we excel at? (the internal business perspective)
- How can we continue to innovate and create value? (the innovation and learning perspective)

The scorecard is balanced because it addresses financial and non-financial perspectives, internal and external perspectives, and short- and long-term perspectives. By answering these four fundamental questions and attaching specific, measurable, achievable, realistic targets (SMART) to them, management is also forced to make the organisation's strategies explicit.

Communicating and driving strategy

Measures undoubtedly influence behaviour. The old adage 'you get what you inspect, not what you expect', is as valid today as it has ever been. Horror stories of poorly designed measures abound. Old-style managers still seek to maximise machine utilisation by making a product that nobody wants to buy. Measures such as the time taken to answer the phone, can lead to operators making lines ring busy, so that customers hang up, rather than hang on. Maliciously or not, employees will tend towards adopting 'gaming tactics' in order to achieve the target performance levels they have been set. Measures send people messages about what matters and how they should behave. When the measures are consistent with the organisation's strategies, they encourage behaviours that are consistent with the strategy. The right measures then not only offer a means of communicating strategy, but also a means of encouraging implementation.

Checking implementation of strategy

Of course the value of measurement does not end with the communication of strategy. For if the right measures have been adopted then they allow management to track progress towards the implementation of strategy. No longer do managers have to rely solely on financial measures that bear little relationship to the strategies they are pursuing today. In the vast majority of organisations financial performance today is largely a function of the strategies that were implemented two or three years ago. In a capital intensive manufacturing business, today's return on investment is largely determined by what value has been extracted over the last 12 months from capital equipment that has been purchased and implemented over a period or 5, 10 or even 15 years. Similarly sales turnover today is a function of last year's customer satisfaction. A downturn in customer satisfaction will not necessarily hit sales in the short term, because it takes a while for the message to get out. The downturn could, however, have a significant impact in the medium term. The beauty of the balanced scorecard is that it takes these issues into account. Yes, emphasis is placed on the short-term financial measures (through the financial perspective). But emphasis is also placed on the actions being taken today (through the other three perspectives) that will between them determine financial performance tomorrow. Strategy is all about managing for the short and long term. The balanced scorecard ensures that managers are able to do this because it provides them with the data they need to track whether their strategies for the short and long term are being implemented.

Challenging strategy

Not all strategies that organisations adopt and successfully implement deliver the expected results. Sometimes the wrong strategies are chosen. Sometimes the actions of competitors negate the impact of the strategies. World-class organisations recognise these difficulties and are increasingly seeking to use their measurement data to challenge the very basis of their strategies.

At the core of any strategy is a set of linked assumptions. In a manufacturing business, for example, it might be assumed that the reason few repeat orders are received is that customers are not happy. It may also be assumed that the reason customers are not happy is that delivery performance is poor. The reason delivery performance is poor may be that everything has to be made to forecast because the manufacturing leadtimes are too long. The reason for long manufacturing leadtimes might be large batch sizes. The reason that large batch sizes are required might be that set-up times are too long. Hence one of the strategies for this business would be to increase manufacturing flexibility through the reduction of set-up times. This would allow batch sizes to be reduced, hence leadtimes would come down, the need to forecast would be eliminated, everything could be made to order and delivery performance should improve.

At the point of implementation this strategy is based on a set of untested assumptions. The measurement data offers an excellent resource to test these assumptions. If the measurement data show that set-up times have been reduced, that batch sizes have been decreased, but that leadtimes have not come down, then one has to question whether the reason why leadtimes are long is that batch sizes are too big. Maybe the reason leadtimes are too long is that the organisation's scheduling systems are ineffective. Maybe the problem is that the manufacturing processes are not capable, hence too much scrap is being produced and too much rework is clogging up the factory. In any event viewing the measurement data holistically allows the assumptions inherent in the organisation's strategies to be challenged. If the strategies are being implemented, but the expected results are not being achieved, then one has to ask whether the strategy is wrong.

3. Is getting the measure going to help me?

Think about the performance measures you see and ask yourself the following questions:

- Do we have a balanced mix of financial and non-financial measures that really reflect our strategies?

- Do our measures encourage people to do the things we want them to do?

- Do our measures help us to understand whether our strategies are right, as well as whether they are being implemented?

- Do we have a systematic process for reviewing our performance and ensuring that we act upon the insights our data provide?

If you have answered yes to all of the questions then this book may have little to offer you. If you have answered no to any of them, then it could be time to review and improve your performance measures. *Getting the measure of your business* provides a structured set of tools and techniques designed to help you do this.

4. Why I should take this approach?

There are many books written on strategy and performance measurement expounding different theories and frameworks. There are very few manuals which tell you precisely how to set your business objectives or how to design and implement your measures. Still fewer that have been extensively tried and tested in real organisations.

This book is all about 'how to do it'.

Why we take a process approach

Nobody, however expert they may be, can come into your business and tell you what you should be measuring.

There are two reasons for this.

- It is unlikely that anyone not closely involved with the business can have sufficient understanding to identify the key measures

- Even if you are given a set of measures, without an understanding of why you are measuring those specific aspects of performance their implementation and use will be flawed

We believe that the people who know most about your business are the people who are currently running it. What is needed is a process for extracting this knowledge and organising it in a way which can be used to design and implement a performance measurement system.

The process has benefits:

- It elicits information from each and every member of the senior management team

- It makes you clarify and quantify what you are trying to achieve

- It creates a common view of the business, the challenges and the key objectives

- It generates commitment to go on to implement the measures

What is a process?

In this context, the process for designing and implementing performance measures has four elements:

- Point of entry (or launch) – this is how the design and implementation of performance measures is introduced to the business

- Participation – this is who should be involved in the workshops

- Procedures – these are the set of tools and techniques which the management team work through together as a group during the workshops

- Project management – this is the administration support, facilitation and co-ordination required to progress the project

This book explains

- How the project should be launched (see Section 3)

- Who should be involved and how long it takes (see Section 1)

- What the tools are, how they are used, including tips, advice and examples (see Section 4 and the CD ROM resource for in-depth guidance)
- How the project should be managed (see Sections 2 and 3)

Application

At the time of this publication, the authors have applied this approach at in excess of 30 different organisations. These range from large divisions of publicly quoted corporations to smaller privately owned businesses. And it works. Not only have the authors used the process, but they have trained other facilitators in the use of the process, and it works for them as well. This book is a manual which you should be able to adopt and put to use in your business.

5. What I should read next?

CEOs

If you are a CEO trying to get an overview of the process, then you should read Section 1, the process overview and possibly scan through the tools in Section 4, the main description of the process. If you then think the process is worth following, key aspects of project management and selecting a facilitator are discussed in Section 2.

Senior managers

If you are a member of the senior management team about to embark on this project, what you have read is probably sufficient. If you want to know more about what is involved and how long it will take, then Section 1 (and especially the summary on pages 21 and 22) covers this.

Facilitators

If you are the consultant, facilitator or internal project manager who is tasked with undertaking this, then you need to read the whole book. Probably the best way is to get an initial view by reading through the book once and then focus in on each part of the process in turn. In this respect the CD ROM resource will help you as it contains detailed facilitation advice; catalogues of alternative tools, techniques and performance measures; questionnaires; and electronic versions of many of the working forms, which can be saved, printed and edited on screen.

These icons appear in this book where you may find that the CD resource has a useful bearing on the subject to hand.

Section 1

Process overview

Contents

We recommend that all participants read this section of the introduction before the first process session in which they are involved.

When embarking upon a new venture various questions spring to mind. Chief among these are:

- What is involved?
- How long will it take?
- How much resource will be consumed?
- What benefit will there be?

The purpose of this section is to answer these questions and to explain the principles underlying *Getting the measure of your business,* and so enable participants to gain a common understanding of:

- What performance is and why it should be measured
- The process of performance measurement system design

1.1 What is performance and why measure it?

The terms performance and measurement often mean different things to different people in the same organisation. To make sense of *Getting the measure of your business* it is important that those involved have a common understanding both of the reasons for carrying out the process and the terms involved. There are three important ingredients in a practical definition and understanding of performance measurement:

- What is the purpose of performance measurement?
- What do the terms performance and measurement mean?
- What is the scope of a performance measurement system?

Purpose

There can be significant disagreement on the meaning and purpose of performance measurement. Many organisations have obsolete measures of doubtful origin and uncertain aim. Some of which can be counterproductive, even to the extent of encouraging inappropriate behaviours. A good performance measurement system will:

- Contain a balanced mix of financial and non-financial measures
- Help you predict what is about to happen to your business, as well as enable you to understand what has happened
- Encourage your people to do the things you want them to do

- Be an integral part of a systematic process for reviewing the measures and ensuring they stimulate purposeful action

Performance – a definition

Performance measurement is the process of quantifying purposeful action, where the process of quantification is measurement and purposeful action equates with performance.

From a Marketing perspective organisations achieve their goals (that is they perform) by satisfying their customers with greater efficiency and effectiveness than their competitors. Efficiency and effectiveness have specific meanings in this context. Effectiveness refers to the extent to which customer requirements are met, while efficiency is a measure of how economically the firm's resources are used when providing a given level of customer satisfaction.

This is an important point because it not only identifies two fundamental dimensions of performance, but also highlights the fact that there can be internal as well as external reasons for pursuing specific courses of action.

For example, one of the quality-related dimensions of performance is product reliability. In terms of effectiveness, achieving a higher level of product reliability might lead to greater customer satisfaction. In terms of efficiency, it might reduce the costs incurred by the business through decreased field failure and warranty claims. Hence, in a business context, performance can be defined as the efficiency and effectiveness of purposeful action.

Given this definition, three others follow:

- Performance measurement is the process of quantifying the efficiency and effectiveness of purposeful action
- A performance measure is an indicator used to quantify the efficiency and/or effectiveness of purposeful action
- A performance measurement system is the set of indicators used to quantify the efficiency and effectiveness of purposeful actions

These definitions highlight the fact that a performance measurement system can be examined at three different levels:

- The individual measures of performance
- The performance measurement system as a whole
- The relationship between the performance measurement system and the environment within which it operates

Each of these levels raises different issues which have to be tackled during the design and implementation of a performance measurement system.

1.2 What does a performance measurement system include?

The individual measures of performance

- Which performance measures should be adopted and why?
- Should any of our existing performance measures be discontinued? If so, which ones and why?
- Are our performance measures cost effective?
- How much does it cost us to collect the data?
- What benefit does the measure provide?

The performance measurement system

- How many measures should the system contain?
- What is the appropriate balance of internal and external, and financial and non-financial measures?
- How can the measures be integrated, both across the organisation's hierarchy and along the business processes?
- How can the problem of conflicting performance measures be resolved?

The broader organisational environment

- How can the performance measures be matched with the firm's strategies?
- How can the performance measures be matched with, used to change, the firm's culture?
- How can the performance measures be matched with the firm's existing recognition and reward schemes?

  Remember
  Performance measurement is a means to an end, not an end in itself. The real benefits of performance measurement come from closing the management loop – ensuring that the measures stimulate appropriate improvements in business performance.
  The next few pages summarise the process of performance measurement system design. (We begin with the most fundamental aspect)

- The purpose or reason(s) for engaging in the process
- A description of the procedure
- Aspects of participation, including the facilitation role
- Process and project management
- Where should you start? What will be your point of entry?

1.3 The performance measurement system design process

A process is a method of operation – the means by which inputs are converted into outputs.

During the process of designing a performance measurement system, inputs such as the organisational context, the nature of the market place and the business strategy have to be considered, while the questions raised above in *What does a performance measurement system include?* are tackled.

Upon completion of the process, a set of measures has to be implemented, which, if used properly, will stimulate improvements in business performance.

At the heart of this process is a procedure – a set of logical steps. Experience has shown that, in the context of performance measurement, this procedure is best divided into two phases, each of which consists of five parts:

Phase 1 (identifying, designing and implementing the top-level performance measures).
Part 1 – What are our main customer-product groups?
Part 2 – What are our business objectives?
Part 3 – Are we achieving our business objectives?
Part 4 – Have we chosen the right measures?
Part 5 – Using our measures to manage the business.

Phase 2 (cascading the top-level measures and identifying appropriate lower-level performance measures)
Part 6 – What can we use to drive performance towards our objectives?
Part 7 – Which performance drivers are the most important?
Part 8 – How do we know these drivers are working?
Part 9 – Have we chosen the right measures for the drivers?
Part 10 – Using these measures to drive business performance.

The words process and procedure are often seen as synonymous. In reality the procedure – how the performance measurement system is actually designed – is only one element of the process. The others are:

- Purpose: why is the management team engaging in the process?
- Participation: who should be involved and at what stage?
- Project management: how, and by whom, should the project be managed?

Purpose

The reasons why management groups engage in the process of designing a performance measurement system vary widely. One group with which we have worked sought to:

Develop an integrated set of strategic performance measures which can be used both to monitor and stimulate appropriate improvements in business unit performance.

Another aimed to:

Develop a mechanism for tracking competitor performance.

While yet another wanted to:

Use the process to change the way people think.

It is vital that the rationale for entering the process is made explicit at the outset. If it is not, project management becomes difficult.

1.4 Procedure – Phase 1

Phase 1 of the procedure is concerned with the identification, design and implementation of the top-level performance measures. Once you have completed Phase 1 you will have:

- Identified the objectives of your business

- Established how to measure progress towards the attainment of these objectives

- Implemented a formal review process to ensure that the insight your measures provide is acted upon

Part 1. What are our main customer-product groups?

The first step is to group your products according to why customers buy them. The reason for this is that businesses often have different objectives for different customer-product groups. You might, for example, wish to milk some groups, while you grow others. If this is the case you will need different measures of performance for the different customer-product groups.

Customer-product grouping is normally a fairly simple task. Often businesses already know their customer-product groups and hence need to do little work to complete Part 1. If, however, you are not sure of your customer-product groups, or wish to check you have identified the right groups, Part 1 will take a little longer.

Typically Part 1:
- Involves the facilitator and representatives from Sales and Marketing as a minimum (usually the senior management team)
- Takes between one and four hours to complete

On completion of Part 1 you will have:

- A clear and shared view of your customer-product groups
- A summary of readily available data which can be used to prioritise attention and action
- A wider and growing understanding among participants of the business

Part 2. What are our business objectives?

Part 2 involves defining a balanced set of business objectives for each of your customer-product groups. When doing this you are encouraged to consider both your own needs, and those of your customers and other stakeholders. You should be aware that blending these, often different, sets of needs is a painful, but extremely valuable, process.

Typically Part 2:
- Involves the facilitator and the entire senior management team
- Takes between two and three hours to complete for the first customer-product group and one hour for each subsequent group

On completion of Part 2 you will have defined for each customer-product group:

- What needs to be improved
- By how much it needs to be improved
- By when this improvement should have been achieved
- Who can contribute to the attainment of these improvements
- What performance measures you require for you to be able to assess your progress

Part 3. Are we achieving our business objectives?

This part is where you will begin to answer whether your business objectives are being achieved by designing and agreeing performance measures. When most people talk about performance measures they tend to mention only two things:

- The title of the measure
- How it will be calculated – the formula

There is, however, much more to performance measurement. Part 3 encourages you to think through these wider issues, especially those to do with closing the management loop – ensuring the measures are designed so that they stimulate appropriate behaviours.

Typically Part 3:
- Involves the facilitator meeting with individual members of the senior management team (one person per performance measure)

- Takes between half an hour and one hour per measure

On completion of Part 3 you will have:

- Formally documented your top-level performance measures
- Identified who should be responsible for managing performance improvement
- Defined what they should do if performance does not appear to be improving
- Checked that your top-level measures will encourage appropriate behaviours

Part 4. Have we chosen the right measures?

Once the top-level performance measures have been developed they have to be signed off. To do this all of the proposed measures have to be reviewed.

Typically Part 4:
- Involves the facilitator and the entire senior management team
- Takes between two and three hours

Upon completion of Part 4 you will have:

- Established that the entire senior management team agrees with the proposed performance measures
- Established a process for reviewing progress on the implementation of the measures
- Established whether there are any barriers to implementation and, if so, what can be done about them

It is rare that complete agreement is reached at the first attempt – expect to repeat this meeting.

Part 5. Using our measures to manage the business

Once the top-level performance measures have been signed off they have to be embedded. It is at this point that the process for reviewing and acting upon the measures is agreed.

Typically Part 5:
- Involves the facilitator and the entire senior management team
- Takes two or three meetings, each of which lasts between two and three hours

Upon completion of Part 5 you will have:

- Agreed an agenda for future performance reviews
- Held a couple of performance review meetings to iron out any teething problems
- Become confident that the measures you have chosen can be used to drive improvements in business performance

1.5 Procedure – Phase 2

Phase 2 of the procedure is concerned with cascading the top-level measures *to identify* appropriate lower-level performance measures. Once you have completed Phase 2 you will have:

- Explained to the people involved what the objectives of your business are and how you are measuring progress
- Helped the people involved identify what they can do at a local level to improve business performance
- Enabled these people to develop and implement local-level measures to assess their own performance

Part 6. What can we use to drive performance towards our objectives?

The top-level performance measures defined and implemented as a result of Phase 1 provide an indication of where the business wants to go. For the business to get there, the activities of all of its people must support these aims. The aim of Part 6 is to explore how the various teams, which together constitute the business, might help the business achieve its aims.

Typically Part 6:
- Involves the facilitator and all the members of a business team (e.g. sales team, manufacturing cell)
- Takes between two and three hours to complete, per team

Upon completion of Part 6 you will have:
- Explained the objectives of your business to your key teams
- Enabled the members of these teams to identify what they can do to ensure business performance improves
- Helped the members of these teams to identify how they might measure their contribution

Part 7. Which performance drivers are the most important?

Once Part 6 has been completed a whole host of activities, that appear to be supportive of the business objectives, will have been identified. The aim of Part 7 is to separate these activities into two categories: the nice-to-do and the must-do.

Typically Part 7:
- Involves the facilitator and all the members of a business team (e.g. sales team, manufacturing cell)
- Takes between two and three hours to complete, per team

Upon completion of Part 7 you will have:
- Enabled the members of the team to prioritise what they should do to ensure business performance improves

Part 8. How do we know these drivers are working?

Once the must-do activities (the key business drivers) have been identified, performance measures to assess progress should be defined. Basically, Part 8 is the same as Part 3, but this time involves the business teams and focuses on the key drivers.

Typically Part 8:
- Involves the facilitator meeting with individual members of each business team (one person per performance measure)
- Takes between half an hour and one hour per measure

Upon completion of Part 8 you will have:
- Formally documented your performance measures for your key drivers
- Identified who should be responsible for managing performance improvement
- Defined what they should do if performance does not appear to be improving
- Checked that the measures will encourage appropriate behaviours

Part 9. Have we chosen the right measures for the drivers?

Basically Part 9 is the same as Part 4, but this time involves the business teams and focuses on the key drivers.

Typically Part 9:
- Involves the facilitator and all the members of a business team (e.g. sales team, manufacturing cell)
- Takes between two and three hours to complete, per team

Upon completion of Part 9 you will have:
- Established that each business team agrees with the proposed performance measures

- Checked that the set of measures that is being proposed is comprehensive
- Identified (and eliminated when possible) any conflicts between the different measures
- Established whether there are any barriers to implementation and, if so, what can be done about them

Part 10. Using these measures to drive business performance

Part 10 is much the same as Part 5, but this time involves the business teams and focuses on the key drivers.

Typically Part 10:

- Involves the facilitator and all the members of a business team (e.g. sales team, manufacturing cell)
- Takes two or three meetings (per team), each of which lasts between two and three hours

Upon completion of Part 10 you will have:

- Agreed an agenda for future performance reviews
- Held a couple of performance review meetings to iron out any teething problems
- Become confident that the measures each business team has chosen really can be used to drive improvements in business performance

1.6 Summaries of the phases of the procedure

Table 1 Summary of Phase 1 of the procedure

Phase 1 Aims	Identify the objectives of your business. Establish how to measure progress towards the attainment of these objectives. Implement a formal review process to ensure that the insight your measures provide is acted upon.		
	Aim	Who is involved	Time needed
Part 1	To identify customer-product groups with distinct competitive requirements.	The facilitator. Representatives from Sales and Marketing.	1–4 hours
Part 2	To agree business objectives for each customer-product group. To agree who can contribute to achieving the objectives and when they should be achieved. To agree what performance measures are required for each of the objectives.	The facilitator. The entire senior management team.	2–3 hours for the first product group. 1 hour for subsequent groups.
Part 3	To define a performance measure for each business object. To identify who is responsible for managing improvement for each business objective and agree what they should do if performance does not improve. To check the measures encourage appropriate behaviour.	The facilitator. Individual members of the senior management team (one person per performance measure).	$\frac{1}{2}$–1 hour for each measure.
Part 4	To check that everyone agrees with all the top-level performance measures. To establish a process for reviewing progress. To check whether there are any barriers to implementation.	The facilitator. The entire senior management team.	2–3 hours.
Part 5	To agree an agenda for future performance reviews. To conduct successful performance reviews.	The facilitator. The entire senior management team.	Two or three meetings, each of which lasts 2–3 hours.

Table 1 Summary of Phase 2 of the procedure

Phase 2 Aims	Explain to your people what the objectives of your business are and how you are measuring progress. Help your people identify what they can do at a local level to improve business performance. Enable your people to develop and implement local-level measure to assess their own performance.		
	Aim	Who is involved	Time needed
Part 6	To communicate your business objectives to your key teams and help them identify how they can help achieve these objectives and how they might measure their contribution.	The facilitator. All members of a business team (e.g. sales team, manufacturing cell).	2–3 hours
Part 7	To enable team members to prioritise what they can do to ensure business performance improves.	The facilitator. All members of a business team (e.g. sales team, manufacturing cell).	2–3 hours for each team.
Part 8	To identify and document a performance measure for each key driver. To agree who is responsible for managing improvements in performance for each key driver and what they should do if performance does not improve. To check that the performance measures encourage appropriate behaviour.	The facilitator. Individual members of a business team (one person per performance measure)	$\frac{1}{2}$–1 hour for each measure.
Part 9	To check that all members of each business team agree with all the performance measures that their team will use. To check that the set of measures is comprehensive and identify (and eliminate) any conflicts between the measures and, finally, whether there are any barriers to implementation.	The facilitator. All members of a business team (e.g. sales team, manufacturing cell).	2–3 hours for each team.
Part 10	To agree an agenda for future performance reviews. To conduct successful performance reviews.	The facilitator. All members of a business team (e.g. sales team, manufacturing cell).	Two or three meetings, each of which lasts 2–3 hours.

1.7 Participation

Who within the company should be involved in the process? (internal participation). Do you need anyone from outside the company? (external participation).

Internal participation

As shown in the summaries (pages 21–22), the performance measurement system design process requires broad participation. A major benefit of the process is the learning that involvement brings. Experience has taught us:

- The senior management team must commit time to the project, working together through the workshops. The CEO's absence, for instance, would signal that the project is unimportant, so if the CEO is not prepared to participate our advice would be not to start the project.

- This process cannot be delegated to a staff team. If the senior management team do not share the insights gained by undertaking the exercise themselves they will tend to criticise the results without a full appreciation of the thinking behind them, thus undermining the enthusiasm of the staff team.

- Finally, the whole senior management team needs to be present for the following reasons:

  Participation in the debate creates an understanding which is lost if individual members are absent.

  Participation creates the commitment to implement the measures and is lost if members are absent.

  Anyone deemed worthy of being a member of the senior management team will have valuable input. If their input and individual perspectives are not available this will reduce the quality of debate and may lead to problems during implementation.

  The implementation of measures is not trivial and requires commitment and dedication. Building team understanding and commitment through engagement in the process are key steps in developing a set of performance measures which have a chance of being implemented and used. There the engagement of the whole senior management team is essential.

External participation

External participants are often useful as they provide a different viewpoint. Typically they include consultants, academics, or corporate staff.

In this process, as in many, a key participant is the facilitator. The fundamental task of the facilitator is to guide the other participants through the process. A facilitator can be a consultant, an academic or a member of the firm's management team. To ensure a successful process, the facilitator must have a number of qualities including:

- Acceptability to the other participants. Being seen as having no axe to grind.

- A participative, democratic style and approach to people.

- A strong identification with the success of the process as defined by the purpose of the project.

There are advantages to using external participants because they generally arrive without the assumptions that members of the business unit carry and are more likely to be experienced in the process.

However, it is in the interests of the company to nominate an internal facilitator to learn from the external facilitator to ensure that the business retains the knowledge captured during, and upon completion of, the process.

1.8 Process and project management

Successful application of the process requires the definition of:

- A clear purpose
- Identified and adequate participation
- A project plan and a management or steering group who will manage the plan

It is usual for the management team of the business to manage the project and a director to own it. The role requiring particular attention is that of the facilitator who, if not experienced in the process, is likely to require training at the outset.

1.9 Launching the process

Four key aspects need to be addressed prior to launching the process:

- A clear definition of the purpose of the project which addresses the question: why are we engaging in this process of performance measurement system design?
- A statement of how this project will be managed
- The identification of an facilitator
- An initial project plan

Once these four key aspects have been established, you are ready to start the process with Phase 1 of the workbook. The next section – Section 2 – offers some guidance on selecting an appropriate facilitator.

1.10 Further reading

Bourne, M. C. S. and Bourne, P. A., (2000) *Understanding the Balanced Scorecard in a Week*, Hodder and Stoughton, London.

Dixon, J. R., Nanni, A. J. and Vollmann, T. E., (1990) *The New Performance Challenge – Measuring Operations for World-Class Competition*, Dow Jones-Irwin, Homewood, Illinois.

Fitzgerald, L., Johnston, R., Brignall, S., Silvestro, R. and Voss, C., (1991) *Performance Measurement in Service Business*, CIMA, London.

Geanuracos, J. and Meiklejohn, I., (1993), *Performance Measurement: The New Agenda, Business Intelligence*, London.

Kaplan, R. S. and Norton, D. P., (1996) *The Balanced Scorecard: Translating Strategy Into Action*, Harvard Business School Press, Boston.

Lynch, R. L. and Cross, K. F., (1991) *Measure Up – The Essential Guide to Measuring Business Performance*, Mandarin, London.

Neely, A. D., (1998) *Measuring Business Performance*, Economist Books, London.

Olve, N. G., Roy, J. and Wetter, M., (1999) *Performance Drivers: A Practical Guide to Using Balanced Scorecard*, John Wiley and Sons, London.

Section 2

Selecting a facilitator

Aim	*To select a facilitator*
Why	The approach needs a facilitator to guide the management team and other supporting staff.
How	**Understanding the role** **Evaluating the options for your business.** Facilitators may be company staff, external consultants or both.

Understanding the role

The facilitator's role includes four principle elements:

1. Assisting the CEO

It is important that the CEO is seen to fully endorse the approach. Since designing measures can be politically sensitive, the facilitator and sponsoring manager need to establish how best to support the approach and how, if necessary, to control it.

In practice, worries that the approach might run away with itself evaporate quickly and concerns about the potential consequences of the project for individuals are allayed as experience of the approach is gained.

2. Understanding the approach.

The facilitator will be asked questions about the approach:

- Why are we doing this part?
- Why are we doing it this way?

The workbook section contains explicit answers to many such questions but there is no doubt that an experienced facilitator will inspire more confidence in participants than one facilitating the approach for the first time. The CD resource base includes information and guidance for facilitators, including specific hints, tips and advice based on the authors' practical experience of facilitating this process. (Training courses are available for facilitators).

3. Helping to achieve consensus.

Re-assessing a company's measurement system can be seen as very threatening. A good facilitator will recognise when certain participants are silent or hesitant and he or she will encourage and help them to speak their minds.

The approach is designed to help structure existing knowledge and perceptions into a useful, agreed whole and it is essential for input to come from all participants. What is long term for one manager may be short term for another. A facilitator should recognise such language and interpretation difficulties and defuse disagreements with simple questions, for example: 'How many years do you mean when you say long term?'.

The facilitator needs to:

- Be seen as impartial and non-threatening to other participants
- Have a questioning, objective mind
- Have good interpersonal skills

4. Acting as project manager

The facilitator will need to:

- Schedule workshops
- Prepare materials

- Produce action minutes
- Act as a repository for the information produced by the approach

The repository role is very important. Because of the ongoing nature of the approach, the ability to refer quickly to past decisions and conclusions is essential.

In-house and external facilitators compared

Table 1 summarises the benefits of using in-house facilitators and those of using external facilitators; it also indicates some of the problems with each.

Table 1 In-house and external facilitators compared

	Assisting the CEO	Understanding the approach	Achieving consensus	Project management	Other
In-house facilitators	A known quantity, their integrity is assured. Their knowledge of the people and company issues can be an advantage in helping to select participants.	This is unlikely to be high without training.	Individuals may have facilitation expertise, impartiality and the respect of their colleagues. Their knowledge of company issues can be an advantage. However, they are likely to have an overwhelmingly internal view of the company.	Depending on the individual it may be difficult for them to keep workshops to time and prevent them being postponed. As a repository for the outcomes of the approach, producing minutes and chasing up required action they have an advantage over external facilitators.	
External facilitators	May be an unknown quantity. Will have professional integrity and credibility, but there may still be concerns over confidentiality.	Likely to be a major advantage. External facilitators bring experience of using the approach with other companies.	Will bring facilitation skills and impartiality. Their external eye and experience in other business may also be valuable.	Will be able to impose discipline – time keeping in workshops and focus on the approach. The cost of using external facilitators ensures workshops are not postponed at short notice. As a repository for outcomes there are disadvantages – they are temporary resources.	Wide experience of other businesses. Access to and contacts with other businesses.

Evaluating the options in your business

Much of your choice will depend on the individuals available in your organisation but do not ignore the possibility of using a combination of in-house and external facilitators.

The blend of an external and an internal facilitator can realise many of the advantages of both. The in-company facilitator can work with and learn from the external facilitator and thereby create the necessary skills in-house.

Such an expectation needs to be agreed with the external facilitator in advance as it will involve training the proposed in-house facilitator, including live practice in the approach and follow-up coaching. Since the approach will be used repeatedly, and if companies do not wish to rely on external facilitation, they need to transfer facilitation expertise and knowledge of the approach into their client company.

Tips

Typical internal facilitator profiles:
Name: Craig McKay
Job title: Production engineer
Organisation: Ory Glass UK
Reasons chosen: Facilitation expertise gained in previous company, widely viewed as objective and impartial. Manufacturing director believes he has potential. Later promoted to run an expanding production department.

Name: Ashwin Joshi
Job title: Business development manager
Organisation: Renfrew Price Pumps Ltd
Reasons chosen: Young, ambitious and determined individual. Non-threatening to project team, but willing to chase them.

Name: Geoffrey Collins
Job title: Change agent
Organisation: Fendora Automotive Components Ltd
Reasons chosen: Highly organised, well respected and knowledgeable individual. Ex-manufacturing manager who had taken on the role of organisational change agent. Excellent interpersonal and team-building skills.

Note: These are the profiles of real individuals who have facilitated the process in existing companies. Only the names of individuals and companies have been changed.

Section 3

Launching the process

Aim
To ensure that those who will have to participate in the process of re-engineering your organisation's measurement systems buy-in to the process.

Why
If you are going to derive a set of measures that reflect your organisation's strategies and then use these measures to manage the business it is essential that the people who understand the strategies and will have to use the measures in the future buy-in to the process.

How
By reviewing the measures that already exist in the organisation and identifying their strengths and weaknesses.

Tips
There are numerous different ways of gaining buy-in to the process. This section suggests two methods. An alternative, more comprehensive method, the diagnostic audit is detailed on the accompanying CD as the Performance Measurement questionnaire.

You might also wish to provide the management with a presentation that gives an overview of the entire process as described in the workbook (Section 4).

One of the first things that you will need to do is convince your management team (and indeed yourself) that you have a problem with your existing measurement system. This section contains three tools that you could use to do this.

Do we have a problem? 1

Draw two axes on a sheet of overhead-projector acetate. Label the two extremes of the *x*-axis internal focus and external focus, and the two extremes of the *y*-axis financial and non-financial.

Ask each member of the management team to identify the single performance measure they review most regularly and where they would position it on the graph. Repeat this process until it becomes obvious whether or not your measurement system is balanced.

Do we have a problem? 2

Give all members of the management team ten Post-it® notes and ask them to record:

- The five best things about the organisation's performance measurement system as it is today

- The five worst things about the organisation's performance measurement system as it is today

Invite members of the team (in increasing order of seniority) to stick their Post-its® on a sheet of flipchart paper, justifying what they have said.

As they are doing so, record the common themes: these will provide guidance on what the ideal measurement system for the business will look like. End the session by checking whether all of the important common themes have been identified and make the point that these are the criteria the management team should use to assess progress. You need to allow about two hours for this session.

Experience shows that this process is extremely valuable, not only because it encourages the management team to think about performance measurement and what they want from the project, but also because it ensures everyone participates in the discussion.

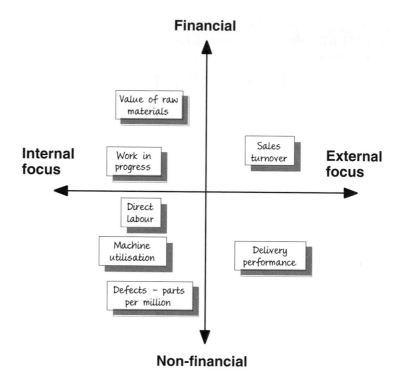

Do we have a problem? 3

Get all members of the management team to do the performance measurement questionnaire on the CD. Analyse the data and present the results back to them showing where the greatest areas of concern are.

Section 4

The workbook

Contents

Phase 1

Introduction, putting Phase 1 in context

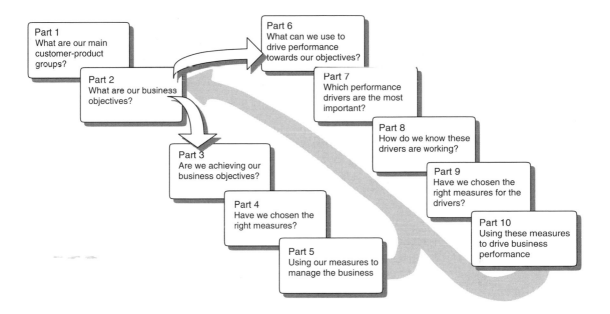

Part 1
What are our main customer-product groups?

Part 2
What are our business objectives?

Part 3
Are we achieving our business objectives?

Part 4
Have we chosen the right measures?

Part 5
Using our measures to manage the business

Part 6
What can we use to drive performance towards our objectives?

Part 7
Which performance drivers are the most important?

Part 8
How do we know these drivers are working?

Part 9
Have we chosen the right measures for the drivers?

Part 10
Using these measures to drive business performance

Some common concerns
- 'We measure everything that walks and moves, but nothing that matters.'
- 'We use 2% of what we measure, the rest is just to cover backs.'
- 'We measure the wrong things to four decimal places of accuracy.'
- 'If you want to know what my inventory levels are now, come back in six weeks.'
- 'We are masters of the micro – we measure paper clip acquisition times.'
- 'Paralysis, but no analysis is the reality of today.'

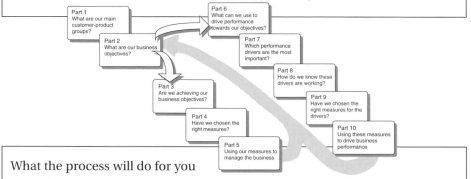

Part 1
What are our main customer-product groups?

Part 2
What are our business objectives?

Part 3
Are we achieving our business objectives?

Part 4
Have we chosen the right measures?

Part 5
Using our measures to manage the business

Part 6
What can we use to drive performance towards our objectives?

Part 7
Which performance drivers are the most important?

Part 8
How do we know these drivers are working?

Part 9
Have we chosen the right measures for the drivers?

Part 10
Using these measures to drive business performance

What the process will do for you

This section of *Getting the measure of your business* describes a process – a practical set of tools and techniques – designed to help you identify, design and implement a balanced set of performance measures that:

- Are consistent with the objectives of your business
- Help you, and your people, identify how business performance can be improved

This section of *Getting the measure of your business* consist of two phases. Phase 1 explains how to identify, design and implement the top-level performance measures for your business. Typically, these top-level measures are reviewed by the board and are designed to provide a balanced picture of the health of the business. Phase 2 describes how you can cascade the top-level measures through the organisation and encourage local groups to develop appropriate action plans and local performance measures.

Both phases are built around a series of worksheets. In the first instance, we would recommend that you concentrate on Phase 1 as this is designed to ensure a relatively quick payback. Once you are confident that you have identified and implemented the appropriate top-level performance measures, you can consider tackling Phase 2.

Phases 1 and 2 each consist of five parts. The order in which the parts are presented is that which seems most logical and generally appropriate to the majority of businesses. However different organisations may choose to re-arrange the order in which they follow the process, tailoring it to suit their particular situation. Furthermore, if you feel you already have the information called for in a particular part, that part may, with care, be omitted.

Part 1
What are our main customer-product groups?

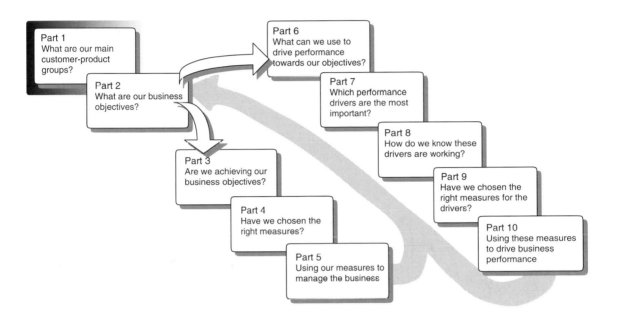

Part 1
What are our main customer-product groups?

Part 2
What are our business objectives?

Part 6
What can we use to drive performance towards our objectives?

Part 7
Which performance drivers are the most important?

Part 3
Are we achieving our business objectives?

Part 8
How do we know these drivers are working?

Part 4
Have we chosen the right measures?

Part 9
Have we chosen the right measures for the drivers?

Part 5
Using our measures to manage the business

Part 10
Using these measures to drive business performance

Aim   *To identify customer-product groups with distinct competitive requirements*

Why
- A single business usually serves several customer-product groups which have different competitive requirements. The performance measurement system needs to measure how well customer requirements are being met and so should be designed to reflect the main groups.

- It is unlikely that all customer-product groups will be equally important to the business. Segmentation will help to decide priorities.

- Discussing the different market requirements creates a debate about what are the important competitive criteria for the company. Identifying and agreeing the groups builds a common picture on which the management team can build throughout the process.

How   By answering the following:

- Does our range of products sell into different markets?

- Does our range of products sell through different distribution channels?

- Do we supply very different customers with different needs?

Work with the Marketing and Sales functions to group products and ignore the way your Operations and/or Manufacturing is currently configured.

Tips   **Typical customer-product groups are:**

- Standard products (often the high volume group).

- Customised or configured to order (more flexible products, medium volume).

- Customer special (designed for a customer's particular need, often low volume, but when high volume, products in this group can resemble standard products).

Most enterprises have only one or two of these groups, but even small subcontract manufacturing enterprises often make own-design products distributed to a range of customers as well as customer-specific items.

Medium to large companies have often identified customer-product groups already in their accounting systems and/or their organisation's structure.

Examples of customer-product groupings

Disc brakepad manufacturer
Products for car assemblers (e.g. Ford, Toyota)
Own-brand replacement parts for garages/DIY outlets
Replacement parts for third-party branding and distribution

Subcontract manufacturer
Subcontract manufacture
Own-design, own-brand medical products
Repair of medical valves

Toiletry goods manufacturer
Own-brand for high-street multiples
Own-brand for local chemists, etc.
High-street multiple branded toiletries (e.g. Marks and Spencer)

Aim *To identify customer-product groups*

How Gather together representatives from Sales and Marketing.

Ask them to brainstorm the main reasons why your customers buy from you.

Take your top 20 products by value and identify the top three reasons why the customers buy each product.

Group the products according to the reasons why customers buy them as shown in Form 1, example right. (A blank form is given on the next page.)

Tips **How many customer-product groups?**

Ideally, you should end up with between two and four distinct groups. Less than two suggests you are not being sensitive enough to market differences. More than four will make developing the performance measurement system very complex. Once you have a reasonable set of customer-product groups (one – four) stick with them. Do not be tempted to add extra complexity by continually subdividing customer-product groups.

There is no one right answer to identifying groups and it may be useful to experiment with alternatives before choosing one to work with. However, one good criteria against which to judge the result is 'does it give the management team new insights into the customer requirements placed on the business?'

Order winning, order qualifying

It can be useful to distinguish between order winning criteria (i.e. those factors that actually win you orders) and order qualifying criteria (i.e. those factors that simply allow you to qualify for business).

For example, companies in the aerospace or pharmaceutical markets must have rigorous quality systems and very high quality conformance. These qualify companies for their market – orders are won on other factors like specification or price.

Finally, customer-product grouping is not an exact science. The aim of this step is to encourage you to think about the products you offer and the customers you serve.

Product	√ Desirable √√ Important √√√ Critical							Customer-product group
	ex stock delivery	reliability	confor- mance	price	hi spec			
p1	√√		√√	√√√				1
p2		√√	√√	√	√√			2
p3	√√		√√	√√√				1
p4		√√	√√	√	√√			2
p5	√√		√√	√√√				1
p6	√√		√√	√√√				1

Form 1 Reasons why customers purchase from us

Form 1. Reasons why customers purchase from us

Product	√ Desirable √√ Important √√√ Critical									Customer-product group

Use version of Form 1 on the CD.

Aim   *To collect data on identified customer-product groups*

Why   To pool knowledge about the business.

How   Complete as much of Form 2 as possible, see example on the right. A blank form is shown on the next page.

Sales as a percentage of total sales is normally easy to collect but it means little without measures of contribution.

Contribution as a percentage of total contribution indicates where the majority of profit is arising (as long as that customer-product group does not attract disproportionately high overhead costs).

Contribution as a percentage of group sales indicates the level of profitability from each customer-product group (as long as no group attracts disproportionately high overhead costs).

Market share and competitor ranking indicates the competitive situation. Sales growth is usually shown as a graph over time, but even a judgement (–2 to +2) can be useful to compare groups.

Do not view this independently from market growth since impressive sales growth in a market growing faster than sales may be bad news.

Market growth is also usually shown as a graph over time. Even in the largest companies this can only be an estimate so a scale (–2 to +2) is used here, as for the sales growth.

Product life-cycle indicates how appropriate current products are to market requirements and is a way of identifying new product requirements.

Tips   Many small firms do not know their market share. Such companies should enter their major competitors' names. For subcontract manufacturers the total value of quotes issued may be a reasonable measure of the market the firm is attempting to address, and the total value of business won as a percentage of total quotes indicates their share of the market.

Market growth may not be known or initially accessible to some companies. But competitors' returns are available from Companies House and industry trends are regularly published in the *Financial Times*.

There is also usually an awareness of whether the amount of business is growing, static or declining.

Customer-product group	Sales as a percentage of total sales	Contribution as a percentage of total contribution	Contribution as a percentage of group sales	Market share ranking/number of competitors	Sales growth*	Market growth*	Customer-product group life-cycle**
Standard products	40	33	25	25%, 3 competitors, 35, 25 & 15%	–1	0	mature
Standard design, customisable	40	47	40	20% 4 competitors all at 20%	0	+1	mature
Customer specified	20	20	35	90% 1 competitor	+1	+1	new product entry

* +2 (growing rapidly), +1 (growing), 0 (static), –1 (declining), –2 (declining rapidly).
** New product entry, fast growth, mature, decline, rapid deline.

Growth	Growing rapidly	Growing	Static	–2	Declining rapidly
Score	+2	+1	0	–1	Declining

Form 2 Customer-product group data

Form 2. Customer-product group data

Customer-product group	Sales as a percentage of total sales	Contribution as a percentage of total contribution	Contribution as a percentage of group sales	Market share ranking/number of competitors	Sales growth*	Market growth*	Customer-product group life-cycle**

* +2 (growing rapidly), +1 (growing), 0 (static), −1 (declining), −2 (declining rapidly).
** New product entry, fast growth, mature, decline, rapid deline.

Use version of Form 2 on the CD.

On completing Part 1, you will have:
- A clear and shared view of your customer-product groups.
- A summary of readily available data which can be used to prioritise attention and action.
- A wider and growing understanding of the business among participants.

Part 2
What are our business objectives?

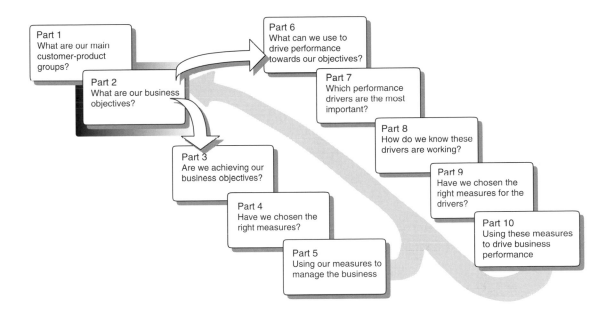

Part 1
What are our main customer-product groups?

Part 2
What are our business objectives?

Part 3
Are we achieving our business objectives?

Part 4
Have we chosen the right measures?

Part 5
Using our measures to manage the business

Part 6
What can we use to drive performance towards our objectives?

Part 7
Which performance drivers are the most important?

Part 8
How do we know these drivers are working?

Part 9
Have we chosen the right measures for the drivers?

Part 10
Using these measures to drive business performance

Aim   *To agree a balanced set of business objectives* for each customer-product group*

Why
- To pool knowledge of the demands placed on the business.
- To represent this knowledge in the form of quantified business objectives.
- To establish what measures are required so that progress towards the objectives can be tracked.

How   **Agree business objectives**

- Identify customer needs: have you considered what your customers want in all the dimensions of quality, time, price (cost) and flexibility?
- Identify other needs: have you considered what the other stakeholders want from the company? (Other stakeholders include: the firm's owners, the management team, other employees, suppliers, the local community and Government.)
- Identify what implications these combined needs have for the business: doing this provides definitions of the broad business objectives.
- Set improvement targets for each business implication.
- Set timescales for the attainment of each target.
- Check whether your business objectives are consistent with any business strategy you might have.

Check that a balanced set of objectives have been developed

- Map the objectives onto a framework and confirm that between them they cover all the key dimensions.

Agree who can contribute to achieving the objectives

- Assess contributions to the attainment of the objectives: split 100 points between the functions according to the contribution they can make.
  Smaller companies may not be functionally organised. Instead of the functions the headings may be the names of the management team.

Agree who will be responsible for developing appropriate measures

---

* Business objectives = business implications + target + timescale (e.g. improve delivery performance by 50% by the end of the financial year).

Aim	*To identify customer needs for each customer-product group, starting with the most important group*
How	The most important customer-product group may not be the biggest but is often the one with the greatest future potential. Allow three hours for the first group and one hour for subsequent ones.

For each customer-product group, answer the following:

- Why do customers buy our products rather than those of our competitors?
- Why will existing customers continue to prefer us in three years time?
- What will make new customers turn to us from existing suppliers?

Tips   **When answering the above questions, is it because:**

Quality
- Our product performs well to specification?
- Our product is outstanding for reliability?

Time
Speed
- We deliver product within the lead time the customer needs?

Reliability
- We always deliver to schedule?

Cost/Price
- We sell at the lowest price?

Flexibility
Range
- We can cope with widely ranging demands?

Response
- We can respond quickly to changing demand?

Innovation
- Our ability to design and manufacture new products quickly?

Other
- We have a long history of good relationships with customers?

Are there other factors that win us orders? If so, these are advantages we will need to protect.

Those who come into contact with customers/markets should be able to give us a view of what is wanted, but let's make sure customers have actually been asked. (This is best done by a third party outside the organisation, if time and resources are available.)

If we have lost any orders, we should ask the customers why.

Make sure we check what our most demanding customers want. What they want today, others will want tomorrow.

It is also important to recognise that there are different types of customer. Immediate customers are those you supply to directly. Intermediate customers are those your customers supply to. Consumers are those who use your products (or the products your components fit into).

Customer needs	Objectives	Stakeholder needs (owners, managers, employees, local community, government, others)
Quality *Very high conformance to specification*		
Time (speed) *Requirement to reduce leadtimes*		
Time (reliability)		
Price (cost) *Low and reducing prices expected*		
Flexibility *Quick response required for new designs*		
Other *Little hard data on customer needs*		

Examples

Quality, time, cost and flexibility can be defined in various different ways, for example:

Quality:

- Performance – the primary operating characteristics.
- Features – optional extras (the bells and whistles).
- Reliability – likelihood of breakdown.
- Conformance – conformance to specification.
- Technical durability – length of time before the product becomes obsolete.
- Serviceability – ease of service
- Aesthetics – look, smell, feel, taste.
- Perceived quality – reputation.
- Value for money.

Time:
Speed:
- Manufacturing lead time.
- Rate of product introduction.
- Delivery lead time.
- Frequency of delivery.
- Speed of quotation

Reliability:
- Due date performance.
- Keeping promises

Price and cost:
- Manufacturing cost.
- Value added.
- Selling price.

- Running cost – cost of keeping the product running.
- Service cost – cost of servicing the product.
- Profit.
- Total lifetime cost

Flexibility
- Material quality – ability to cope with incoming materials of varying quality.
- Output quality – ability to satisfy demand for products of varying quality.
- New product – ability to cope with the introduction of new products.
- Modification – ability to modify existing products.
- Deliverability – ability to change delivery schedules.
- Volume – ability to accept varying demand volumes.
- Product mix – ability to cope with changes in the product mix.
- Resource mix – ability to cope with changes in the resource mix (i.e. the mix of labour, particularly people on short-term contracts).

Form 3. Customer/stakeholder needs and implications for customer-product group

	Customer needs ➤	Objectives ◄	Stakeholder needs (owners, managers, employees, local community, government, others)
Quality			
Time (speed)			
Time (reliability)			
Price (cost)			
Flexibility			
Other			

Use version of Form 3 on the CD.

Aim   *To identify other stakeholder needs for and from each customer-product group*

How   Answer the following:

- Who are our other stakeholders?
- What do the other stakeholders want from the business?

Tips   **Other stakeholders' include:**

Owners: growth, financial performance (return on investment (ROI), return on sales), cash generation, flotation in a year, exit from this product group, to use this group as a cash cow.

Managers: ambitions fulfilled, growth, longevity of the business, personal development.

Employees: job security, longevity of the business, personal development.

Suppliers: stable demand, long term contracts, early involvement in new product introduction.

The local community: employment, a pleasant environment, a feeling of civic pride.

Government: regulatory – health and safety, pollution control, development grants and assistance.

To get the information, why not interview the most relevant stakeholders?

Customer Needs	Objectives	Stakeholder needs (owners, managers, employees, local community, government, others)
Quality Very high conformance to specification		Less scrap
Time (speed) Requirement to reduce lead times		
Time (reliability)		
Price (cost) Low and reducing prices expected		Strict targets on ROI
Flexibility Quick response required for new designs		
Other Little hard data on customer needs		Assure the longevity of the business. Growth. Meet emission regulations.

Form 3 Customer/stakeholder needs and implications for customer-product group

Aim *To identify business objectives*

How Compare, blend and balance the customer and stakeholder needs to answer the following:

- What are the set of objectives which the business should follow that satisfy both customer and other stakeholder needs?

Tips At this stage, people may jump ahead and offer solutions before the implications are clearly defined – they come up with how-to answers rather than what the implications are.

Example

Instead of identifying implications like: 'We need to improve our delivery performance and reduce our cost base'. People may jump straight to a solution such as: 'We need to implement manufacturing cells'.

Such a solution, offered before the implications of customer and stakeholder needs are understood and agreed by all, can leapfrog the discussion and result in an incomplete or erroneous understanding of the needs of the business.

Don't be side-tracked by solutions at this stage, no matter how attractive they seem. But record them on a flipchart and arrange to discuss them at a separate meeting.

Other solutions that might be offered include statements such as;

- 'We should increase the stability of our production processes.'
- 'We should adopt statistical process control.'
- 'We should re-engineer our business.'

Distinguishing between 'whats' and 'hows' is not always easy. Don't get too hung up on semantics, but before writing anything in the implications column ask "Is what I am about to write a solution to a problem?" If the answer is yes, you are about to record a how rather than a what.

Customer Needs	Objectives	Stakeholder needs (owners, managers, employees, local community, government, others)
Quality Very high conformance to specification		Less scrap
Time (speed) Requirement to reduce lead times	Reduce lead time Reduce raw material stocks Reduce work in progress	
Time (reliability)		
Price (cost) Low and reducing prices expected	Ongoing reduction of cost base	Strict targets on ROI
Flexibility Quick response required for new designs	Reduce new product lead time	
Other Little hard data on customer needs	Examine alternative markets	Assure the longevity of the business. Growth. Meet emission regulations.

Form 3 customer/stakeholder needs and implications for customer-product group

Aim   *To check that a balanced set of objectives has been developed*

- Are the objectives that have been identified balanced?
- Do they relate to the internal and external dimensions of performance?
- Do they cover both the financial and non-financial dimensions?
- Do they offer challenges for both the short and long term?

How
- Map the objectives onto the modified balanced scorecard (Form 4) and answer the following questions:
- Is there a reasonable balance between the objectives chosen?
- Have we satisfactorily covered each dimension?

Tips   **Mapping objectives**

The balanced scorecard, originally conceived by Bob Kaplan and David Norton, consists of four key perspectives:

- *Financial* – How do we look to our shareholders?
- *Customer* – How do we look to our customers?
- *Internal* – What must we excel at?
- *Innovation and learning* – What must we do to ensure the business continues to innovate and create value in the future?

Although these four perspectives were the only ones that featured in the original balanced scorecard, it is often worth adding a fifth, namely the *Supplier* perspective. Here the question being addressed is:

- What do we need from our supplier?

Once the previously defined objectives have been mapped onto the modified balanced scorecard (Form 4) then any gaps – i.e. any perspectives not addressed – can be filled through the development of new objectives if necessary.

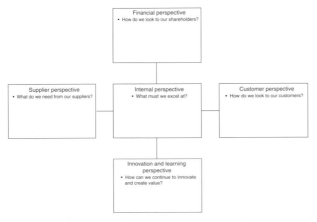

Form 4. Modified balanced scorecard

Form 4. Modified balanced scorecard

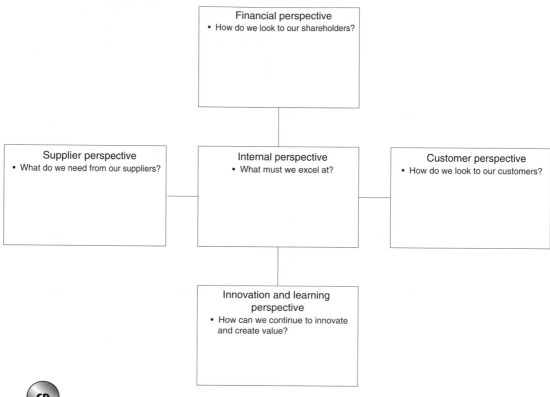

Financial perspective
- How do we look to our shareholders?

Supplier perspective
- What do we need from our suppliers?

Internal perspective
- What must we excel at?

Customer perspective
- How do we look to our customers?

Innovation and learning perspective
- How can we continue to innovate and create value?

Use version of Form 4 on the CD.

Aim   *To agree targets and check against business strategy*

By this stage you should have derived a set of business objectives for each product group, based on the customer and stakeholder needs defined earlier.

First we need to assess the relative priorities of these objectives, then we need to agree improvement targets for each objective and check whether the objectives are consistent with any previously defined business strategy.

How   Answer the following.

- What are the relative priorities of these objectives?
- What, how much and by when should we aim to improve?
- Are the improvements we are proposing consistent with our business strategy?
- If not, do the objectives need to be changed?
- If so, how?

Tips   Share 100 points between the objectives to show their relative priority.

A target only exists if it specifies: how much and by when?

What do we know about our competitors' performance in these areas? This can be important for prioritising our efforts.

In many cases little is known about competitor performance. If you feel you do not know enough to set up appropriate targets, make sure someone leaves the meeting with an action to collect the necessary data.

One useful source of data is the surveys published by the *Financial Times*. These identify industry trends and industry structures.

Objectives				Responsibilities and contributions							Check / develop measure
Description	Priority	Target									
		Improvement	By when?								
Improve delivery reliability	40	95% delivery on time in full	End of this year								
Ongoing reduction of cost base	40	10%	Year on year								
Reduce customer complaints	20	Reduce current level by 50%	Within 6 months								

Form 5. Customer-product group: Precision castings

Form 5. Customer-product group

Objectives				Responsibilities and contributions							Check / develop measure
Description	Priority	Target									
		Improvement	By when?								

Use version of Form 5 on the CD.

Aim   *To assess contributions*

Who, or which functions, have the resources, ability and authority to enable movement towards the targets?

How   Answer the following:

- Who can determine whether the desired improvements are achieved?

Tips   Assessing contribution

This will involve negotiation and discussion amongst all the managers.

Record the percentage or proportion each function can contribute towards achieving each improvement target.

The facilitator must be prepared to push managers for a decision at the start of this process.

The exact percentage each function gets is not important. The purpose of this stage is to get the whole management team to buy-in to the fact that everyone will have to contribute if the objectives are to be achieved.

Note: Depending on the culture of your organisation you may prefer not to use a percentage system and use the following scale instead:

*   supportive effort required

**   medium contribution required

***   high contribution required

Objectives				Responsibilities and Contributions						Check / Develop measure
Description	Priority	Target		Mnf.	Sales	Dev.	Fin.	H.R.	Qual.	
		Improvement	By when?							
Improve delivery reliability	40	95% delivery on time in full	End of this year	60%	20%		10%		10%	
Ongoing reduction of cost base	40	10%	Year on year	50%	10%	20%	5%	10%	5%	
Reduce customer complaints	20	Reduce current level by 50%	Within 6 months	30%	20%	20%	5%	5%	20%	

Form 5. Customer-product group: Precision castings

Aim   *To define responsibilities for checking or developing performance measures for each business objective*

How   Define responsibilities for developing each measure.

For each business objective a suitable performance measure needs to be developed. Each performance measure should be developed by an appropriate, named individual who will report back to the group at a later meeting.

Even when a measure is already available it should be checked to make sure it is appropriate.

The question to be answered for each objective is:

- Who will be responsible for developing an appropriate measure for this business objective?

Put their initials in the right hand column of the business objectives sheet (Check/develop measure), in the appropriate row.

Tips   **Appropriate named individuals**

Individuals responsible for developing measures should be members of the team that has been defining the business objectives.

Objectives					Responsibilities and contributions						Check / develop measure
Description	Priority	Target		Mnf.	Sales	Dev.	Fin.	H.R.	Qual.	
		Improvement	By when?								
Improve delivery reliability	40	95% delivery on time in full	End of this year	60%	20%		10%		10%	NB
Ongoing reduction of cost base	40	10%	Year on year	50%	10%	20%	5%	10%	5%	DR
Reduce customer complaints	20	Reduce current level by 50%	Within 6 months	30%	20%	20%	5%	5%	20%	AN

Form 5. Customer-product group: Precision castings

On completing Part 2, you will have:

- Defined, for each customer-product group:
  - What needs to be improved.
  - By how much it needs to be improved.
  - By when this improvement should have been achieved.
- Identified who can contribute to achieving these improvements.
- Established what performance measures you require to be able to assess progress.
- Established who is going to define each measure.

Part 3
Are we achieving our business objectives?

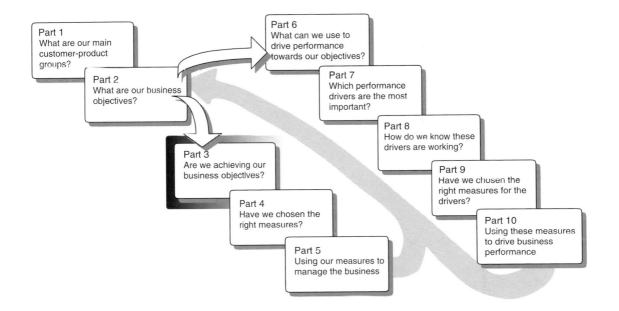

Part 1
What are our main customer-product groups?

Part 2
What are our business objectives?

Part 3
Are we achieving our business objectives?

Part 4
Have we chosen the right measures?

Part 5
Using our measures to manage the business

Part 6
What can we use to drive performance towards our objectives?

Part 7
Which performance drivers are the most important?

Part 8
How do we know these drivers are working?

Part 9
Have we chosen the right measures for the drivers?

Part 10
Using these measures to drive business performance

Aims

To develop a performance measure for each business objective

To complete one performance measure record sheet for each business objective

Why

Defining a performance measure involves more than simply identifying a formula. This step forces you to think through the broader issues involved.

How

Develop a measure for each business objective

The performance measure needs to show:

- How close to (or far from) the target you are
- How quickly you are moving towards the target

It also needs to be designed so that it stimulates:

- Appropriate behaviour
- Managerial action

The headings on the performance measure record sheet (see the example on this page and Form 6 p. 71) may help you in developing the measure.

Complete one performance measure record sheet

Fill in one performance measure record sheet for each measure. This should help you identify the right measures.

    The example on this page shows how this was achieved in one business.

Tips

Work sequentially through the boxes on the performance measure record sheet. Once you have defined the target, the formula should be relatively easy to define. Bear in mind that it is the formula that influences the way people behave.

    Once you have completed the performance measure record sheet, remember to ask: is this measure forward looking? Be prepared to loop around the boxes and keep working on the measure until it is practical and will encourage the behaviour you want.

Measure	Delivery performance
Purpose	To stimulate improvements in our delivery reliability
Relates to	Business implications; delivery on time and minimise overall lead times
Target	z% by end of next year
Formula	$\dfrac{\text{No. of orders delivered in full on the day they were promised}}{\text{Total number of orders}} \times 100$
Frequency	Weekly
Who measures?	A. Smith – production control
Source of data	Due date – as stated on customer schedule. Actual delivery date – by phoning the customer
Who acts on the data?	A. N. Other – manufacturing manager
What do they do?	If performance is improving rapidly enough, nothing. If not, set up manufacturing engineering task force to; (a) investigate why, (b) make recommendations and (c) make appropriate changes
Notes and comments	Measure places equal weighting on early as well as late delivery
Date/issue number	17 February 2000 / issue no. 2

Form 6. Performance measure record sheet

Form 6. Performance measure record sheet – guidance notes

Measure	The title of the measure. A good title is self-explanatory, avoids jargon and explains what the measure is and why it is important.
Purpose	If a measure has no purpose then why introduce it? Example purposes: 1. To enable us to monitor the rate of improvement thereby driving down the total cost. 2. To ensure that ultimately all delayed orders are eliminated. 3. To stimulate improvement in our supplier's delivery performance. 4. To ensure that the new product introduction lead time is continually reduced.
Relates to	Identify the business objectives that the measure relates to. As with 'purpose', if the measure being considered does not relate to any business objective then why introduce it?
Target	Targets specify the levels of performance we need to achieve and the timescales within which we need to achieve them. Example targets: 1. X % improvement year on year. 2. Y % reduction during the next 12 months. 3. Achieve Z % delivery performance (on time, in full) by the end of next year.
Formula	How we measure something will affect the way people behave. An appropriately defined formula should drive people towards good business practice. Beware of any formula that might stimulate behaviour we do not want!
Frequency	The frequency with which performance should be recorded and reported is a function of the importance of the measure and the volume of data available.
Who measures?	This box should identify the person who is to collect and report the data.
Source of data	This box should specify where to get the data from. If we want to see how performance changes over time, then we must get our data from the same source each time.
Who acts on the data?	This box should identify the person who is going to act on the data.
What do they do?	Without some action here, the measure is pointless. We may not be able to detail the action to be taken if the performance proves either acceptable or unacceptable as the detail may depend on the context at the time. We can define in general the management process to be followed in the case of acceptable or unacceptable performance. Examples: 1. Set up a continuous improvement group to identify reasons for poor performance and to make recommendations as to how it can be improved. 2. Publish all performance data and an executive summary on the shopfloor as a way of demonstrating commitment to empowerment. 3. Identify commonly occurring problems. 4. Set up a review team, consisting of Sales, Development and Manufacturing personnel to establish whether alternative materials can be used.
Notes and comments	Any specific features, outstanding issues, specific problems, to do with the measure.
Date/issue number	The date and issue number of the record sheet.

Form 6. Performance measure record sheet

Measure	
Purpose	
Relates to	
Target	
Formula	
Frequency	
Who measures?	
Source of data	
Who acts on the data?	
What do they do?	
Notes and comments	
Date/issue number	

Use version of Form 6 on the CD.

The facilitator should test and review each completed performance measure record sheet by asking:

Measure

What should this measure be called?

Does this title explain what the measure is?

Does it explain why the measure is important?

Is it a title that everyone will understand?

Purpose

Why are you introducing this measure?

What do you want it to do?

Relates to

Which of the business objectives does this measure relate to?

Target

What level of performance do we desire?

How long will it take us to reach this level of performance?

How does this compare with our competitors?

How good are they currently?

How fast are they improving?

Formula

How are we going to measure this dimension of performance?

Can the formula be defined in mathematical terms?

Is it clear?

Does it explain exactly what data are required?

What behaviour will it induce?

Are there any other behaviours that we want it to induce?

Is the scale we are using appropriate?

How accurate will the data generated be?

Are they accurate enough?

If we use an average, how much data will we lose?

Is this acceptable?

Do we need to know the spread of performance?

Frequency

How often should this measure be made?

How often should it be reported?

Will we be able to collect and analyse the data rapidly enough?

How much delay will there be in improving performance along this dimension?

Who measures?

Who, by name, is actually responsible for making this measure?

Source of data

Where will they get the data from?

Who acts on the data?

Who, by name, is actually responsible for ensuring that performance along this dimension improves?

What do they do?

What actions will they be taking to do this?

Tips

A useful concept is that of the perfectly executed order. When defining measures, ask yourself if you are really capturing everything you need to capture. An order can be classified as delivered on time if it arrives at the customer's facility on the day it was promised. Of course this may not be the day the customer originally wanted it. Similarly if the order arrives on time but incomplete, or the invoice overcharges the customer, is it a perfectly executed order?

Once the measure has been defined, ask how practical it is. If it is not going to be practical to collect and analyse the data, try to identify a simpler measure. The trick when designing measures is to adopt the simplest measure you can that is consistent with what you are trying to achieve. Very complex measures become expensive to implement and can lead to problems in terms of time lags.

The facilitator's role

The facilitator's role when a manager is completing a performance measure record sheet is to ask questions like:

- What?
- Who?
- How?
- Where?
- When?

A good facilitator will question everything, because this is really the only way of checking both the logic underlying the measure and its comprehensiveness.

The kind of discussion that results is shown in the example on this page. Here it was found that the original measure was inappropriate.

Example questions listed under the performance measure record sheet headings are shown on the previous page.

Example

(F – facilitator; SM – senior manager)

F   'Why do you measure sales turnover?'

SM 'Because it tells me how well sales are holding up.'

F   'Why do you need to know how well sales are holding up?'

SM 'Because part of my job is to ensure that we meet sales targets.'

F   'Why does a measure of sales turnover help to ensure that you meet your sales targets?'

SM 'Well...it doesn't exactly help me to ensure that we meet our sales targets, but it does help me tell whether we met last month's targets.'

F   'Why do you need to know whether you met last month's sales targets?'

SM 'Because...one of the things we discuss at the board meeting is whether we met last month's sales targets. So it is important for me to know in advance the level of performance we achieved and the reasons for any performance shortfall.'

F   Why don't you discuss next month's anticipated performance at the board
       meeting? Wouldn't a measure of orders received, or quotes submitted be better
       for managing sales turnover?'

Tips   There are a lot of measures, information about types of measures and considerations
             about how to use them in the catalogue of performance measures on the CD
             resource. Updates of this catalogue can be obtained from
             www.cranfield.ac.uk/som/cbp

> ***Upon completing Part 3, you will have:***
> - Formally documented your top-level performance measures.
> - Identified who should be responsible for managing performance improvement.
> - Defined what they should do if performance does not appear to be improving.
> - Checked that your top-level measures will encourage appropriate behaviour.

Part 4
Have we chosen the right measures?

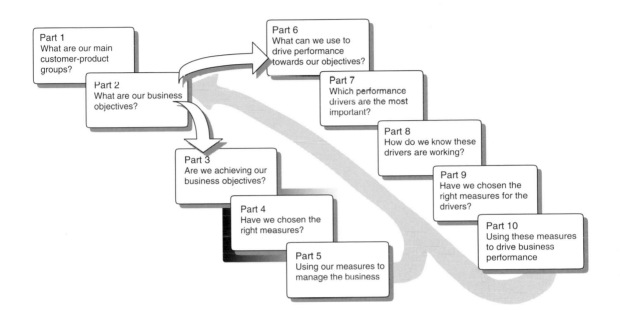

Part 1
What are our main customer-product groups?

Part 2
What are our business objectives?

Part 3
Are we achieving our business objectives?

Part 4
Have we chosen the right measures?

Part 5
Using our measures to manage the business

Part 6
What can we use to drive performance towards our objectives?

Part 7
Which performance drivers are the most important?

Part 8
How do we know these drivers are working?

Part 9
Have we chosen the right measures for the drivers?

Part 10
Using these measures to drive business performance

Aims

To check that everyone agrees with all the top level performance measures

To establish a process for tracking progress with the implementation of each measure

To check whether there are any barriers to implementation

Why

It is now time to take a step back and check you are happy with your top-level performance measures. This is the last chance you will have before you implement them.

How

Check that everyone agrees with all the top-level performance measures. It is likely that each performance measure will have been seen by relatively few people so far. At this stage the rest of the group needs to be given the opportunity to comment.

Check whether there are any barriers to implementation. Are your reward systems consistent with your performance measures? If not, do you need to change your reward systems?

Are there any existing performance measures inconsistent with your new measures? If so, should you discontinue some of your existing measures?

Tips

By the end of this part you should have a formally agreed, balanced set of top-level performance measures. Once Part 4 has been completed the record sheets should be written up neatly and subject to formal change procedures, i.e. once the measures have been agreed at this meeting they should *not* be changed without formal notification.

One way of writing them up neatly is to type their content into electronic versions from the CD resource. These can be printed, saved and amended in future as necessary.

Most forms shown in this book are available as electronic versions on the CD.

Aim   *To check that everyone agrees with all the top level performance measures*

How   Use Form 7 illustrated opposite and included on the CD.

1. Arrange a meeting involving everybody in the senior management team and all the people who have been responsible for developing the performance measures.

2. Invite each person to give a brief presentation explaining the performance measure(s) they have developed.

3. Encourage the audience to pull each measure to pieces and identify whether it is likely to lead to any undesirable behaviours. Useful tests at this stage include:

   - *Truth* – Is it definitely measuring what it is meant to?
   - *Focus* – Is the measure measuring *only* what it is meant to?
   - *Consistency* – Is the measure consistent whenever and whoever measures?
   - *Clarity* – Are the results open to ambiguous interpretation?
   - *Access* – Can the data be readily communicated and easily understood?
   - *'So what?'* – Can, and will, the measure be acted upon?
   - *Cost* – How expensive is it to collect, collate and analyse the data?
   - *Timeliness* – Can the data be collected and analysed quickly enough?
   - *Gaming* – Will the measure encourage undesirable behaviours?

4. After each performance measure has been presented check that everybody agrees with the target as defined on the performance measure record sheet.

5. Nominate someone (a single person) to own the measure. This person (the owner), will be expected in the future to:

   - Keep track of progress on this particular dimension of performance.
   - Propose corrective action plans as and when they are needed.

Tips   When asking people to prepare their presentations limit them to one slide only – the performance measure record sheet.

It is worth trying to make all the necessary modifications at the meeting, although often it will prove necessary to repeat the measures review process, especially for those measures designed to track complex dimensions of performance.

Performance measure	Who will present	Modification required	Target agreed	Owner approved
Delivery reliability	AHR	No	Yes	AHR
Cost base	JFM	Yes – completed	Yes	JFM
Customer complaints	ADN	Redraft by next meeting	No	JGS

Form 7. Sign off

Form 7. Sign off

Performance measure	Who will present	Modification required	Target agreed	Owner approved

Use version of Form 7 on the CD.

Aim *To establish a process for tracking progress with the implementation of each measure*

How Implementation of measures requires the completion of four distinct activities. First the measure must be designed. Then it must be reviewed and accepted. Next the necessary data collection processes have to be established. Finally the measure can be used to manage performance. By this stage of the process all of the top-level measures should have been designed, and a significant number of them will have been accepted, although there may be others that require further work. Use form 8 to capture progress to date with each measure and agree a process for reviewing progress in the future.

Tips While designing measures is intellectually challenging, implementation is often the point at which most measurement initiatives fail. There are numerous reasons for this, but the most significant is that the time and effort required to establish the necessary data capture and collation infrastructure becomes too great.

It is therefore really important to plan at the implementation stage an appropriate review process so that senior management regularly review progress of the implementation effort.

Measure	Owner	Measure designed? (Y/N)	Measure agreed? (Y/N)	Data available? (Y/N)	Measure used (Y/N)
Delivery reliability	AHR	Y	N	Y	N
Cost base	JFN	N	N	N	N
Customer complaints	ADN	N	N	N	N

Form 8 Measure implementation

Form 8. Measure implementation

Measure	Owner	Measure designed? (Y/N)	Measure agreed? (Y/N)	Data available? (Y/N)	Measure used (Y/N)

Use version of Form 8 on the CD.

Aim   *To check if there are any other barriers to implementation*

How   Give each member of the group between six and ten Post-it® notes and ask them:

- To identify, and write down on the Post-it® notes, the three to five things that they think will most hinder the successful introduction of the top-level performance measures (one per Post-it®).

- To identify, and write down on the Post-it® notes, the three to five things that they think will most help the successful introduction of the top-level performance measures (one per Post-it®).

Now invite each member of the group to stick their Post-its® on Form 9 as shown in the example on this page.
   A blank version is shown on the next page.

Then:

- Extract the main barriers to implementation and identify what can be done about them.

- List the factors that will make implementation easier and decide how their impact can be maximised.

Tips   Typical barriers include factors such as: lack of resource, the fact that the organisation's reward systems are inconsistent with the performance measures being proposed, the concern that people may feel threatened by the performance measures.
   Factors that make implementation easier include: the possibility of publishing the measures on notice boards or in a newsletter, the existence of a forum where the performance can be reviewed, the opportunity to link the implementation to an existing initiative, a total quality management programme.

	Factors that will make implementation easier ⇨	Proposed measures ⇦	Factors that will make implementation difficult
Factors that will affect all measures	Publication of results in newsletter		Existing sales incentive scheme
			Fear that the measures will be used as a stick
			Emphasis on machine utilisation
Factors that will affect specific measures		Delivery performance	
		Cost base	
	The link to customer satisfaction programme	Customer complaints	

Form 9. Barriers

Form 9. Barriers

	Factors that will make implementation easier ⇨	Proposed measures ⇦	Factors that will make implementation difficult
Factors that will affect all measures			
Factors that will affect specific measures			

Use version of Form 9 on the CD.

On completing Part 4, you will have:

- Established that the entire senior management team agrees with the proposed performance measures.

- Established an appropriate process for regularly reviewing progress with the implementation of the measures.

- Established whether there are any barriers to implementation and, if so, what can be done about them.

Part 5
Using our measures to manage the business

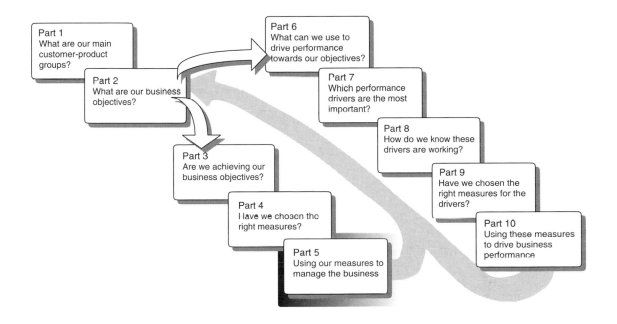

Part 1
What are our main customer-product groups?

Part 2
What are our business objectives?

Part 3
Are we achieving our business objectives?

Part 4
Have we chosen the right measures?

Part 5
Using our measures to manage the business

Part 6
What can we use to drive performance towards our objectives?

Part 7
Which performance drivers are the most important?

Part 8
How do we know these drivers are working?

Part 9
Have we chosen the right measures for the drivers?

Part 10
Using these measures to drive business performance

Facilitation advice

Aims   *To agree an agenda for future performance reviews*

To agree a mechanism for reviewing the performance measurement system

To conduct successful performance reviews

Why   Performance measures are simply a means to an end. All the time and effort you have spent identifying and defining your top-level measures will be wasted unless you establish a review mechanism which ensures that action follows measurement.

How   **Agree an agenda for future performance reviews**

Having finished the formal development of your performance measurement system you now need to agree how you will use the performance measures on an ongoing basis.

To do this you need to address the following questions:

- How will performance be reviewed?
- How frequently will it be reviewed?
- In what forum will it be reviewed?
- Who will be responsible for organising the reviews?
- Who will be involved?
- What will be the agenda?
- When will the first review place?

Agree a mechanism for reviewing the performance measurement system

Performance measurement systems are not static. Rather they evolve as market conditions change and performance improves. Too often new performance measures are introduced, without old ones being deleted.

To avoid this, you need to agree a mechanism that will help you maintain your measurement system on an ongoing basis.

Conduct successful performance reviews

- What makes performance reviews successful in practice?
- What is the role of the chairman?
- What is the role of the facilitator?

Tips   You are likely to find that it will take a couple of review meetings before the group falls into the habit of discussing action plans rather than simply reviewing last month's performance.

One of the jobs of the facilitator is to help the group make this transition.

A simple way of doing this is to keep asking: 'What do you think we should do to help improve performance?'

Aim   *To agree an agenda for future performance reviews*

How   Performance measures are at their most valuable when they stimulate appropriate action. Performance reviews should be structured so that they ensure this happens.

Questions you need to answer at this stage include:

- How will performance be reviewed?
  The key to a good performance review is to have a mechanism that not only enables you to assess how well you have performed, but that also stimulates the production of appropriate corrective action plans. Many firms have found the mechanism developed by Ford Electronics a useful way of doing this.

- How frequently will performance be reviewed and in what forum?
  Performance measures should be reviewed regularly, often on a monthly basis. It is recommended that you do *not* set up a new management meeting to review performance. Instead the performance reviews should become an integral part of an activity that is already ongoing e.g. the board meeting.

- Who will be responsible for organising the reviews?
  The owner of each measure should be responsible for collating the data they need and for presenting them at the review. It is often useful to nominate an overall co-ordinator whose role is to keep the necessary records and take the minutes of the meeting.

- Who will be involved?
  This will be company specific. At the very least, however, the owners of all the performance measures will have to be present.

- What will be on the agenda?
  Typically, the agenda for the review will contain the following items: a review of previous minutes, a review of the top-level performance measures, agreed action plans and any other business.

- When will the first review take place?
  Why not fix a date for the first review meeting now?

Form 10. The Ford visualisation

On the next page, there is the blank form of this chart for photocopying. This page gives a brief description of what data should go into each part of the chart and an example using data from an earlier example in this workbook.

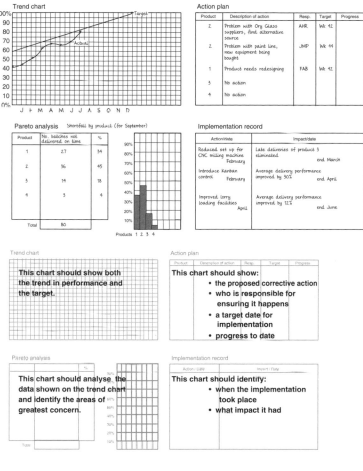

Form 10. The Ford visualisation

Trend chart

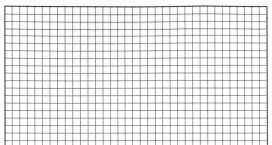

Action plan

Product	Description of action	Resp.*	Target	Progress

Pareto analysis

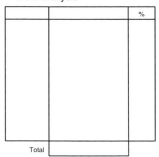

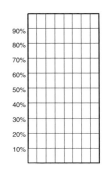

Implementation record

Action/date	Impact/date

---

* Responsible individual's initials.

Aim   *To agree a mechanism for reviewing the performance measurement system*

How   Performance measurement systems are often allowed to expand to the extent that they become unmanageable. So before going live with your performance measurement system, address the following questions:

- Do we have any mechanisms in place to which we could tie a review of the performance measurement system?
- Who will be responsible for ensuring the review takes place?
- How will they go about it?

Tips   Often the review of the performance measurement system is tied to the annual planning cycle. Other options include linking it to the budget cycle or the production of the annual accounts.

Aim   *To conduct successful performance reviews*

How   Always review the last set of minutes.

Review all the top-level performance measures.

Agree actions.

Tips   Get the measures printed on overhead transparencies and projected onto a screen at the review meeting. This focuses everyone's attention on the measure under discussion. Experience has shown that reviewing measures in a reporting pack (where everyone has their own copy) is not as effective as viewing a measure projected on a screen.

Do not be surprised if the first review does not work as well as you had hoped. What tends to happen is that the group's understanding of the review process evolves over time. Initially people tend to use the review as a forum for reporting how well they are doing. Later they begin to understand that what is really required is action plans to improve performance.

To ensure that this group learning takes place it is vital that the chairman and the facilitator continually ask the owner of each measure:

- Are we on course to achieve the target?
- If not, what do you propose we do?

If you decide to publish the measures it is also worth considering copying them onto different coloured pieces of paper. January can be the yellow month, February the red month etc. This provides a visual signal that the data on your notice boards has changed and is up to date.

It is also worth publishing a notice specifying who owns each measure. This is a useful way of signalling senior management commitment and making explicit who is responsible for each dimension of performance.

Note: It is recommended that you concentrate on getting this system up and running before attempting Phase 2 of this process – cascading the measures.

Upon completing Part 5, you will have:

- Agreed an agenda for future performance reviews.
- Held a couple of performance review meetings to iron out any teething problems.
- Become confident that the measures you have chosen really can be used to drive improvements in business performance.

Phase 2

Introduction, putting Phase 2 in context

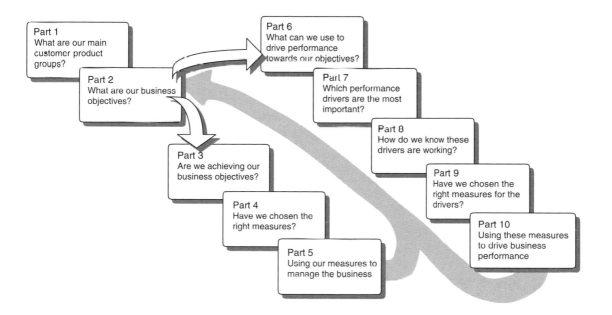

Part 1
What are our main customer product groups?

Part 2
What are our business objectives?

Part 3
Are we achieving our business objectives?

Part 4
Have we chosen the right measures?

Part 5
Using our measures to manage the business

Part 6
What can we use to drive performance towards our objectives?

Part 7
Which performance drivers are the most important?

Part 8
How do we know these drivers are working?

Part 9
Have we chosen the right measures for the drivers?

Part 10
Using these measures to drive business performance

Phase 1

Worked with top management to identify the organisation's top-level objectives, and how to measure progress towards them.

Phase 2

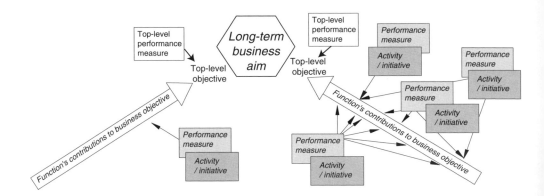

Works at the level of individual teams and functional business units. It looks at what initiatives and activities will enable progress towards achieving the top-level objectives and also how to measure and manage their effectiveness.

Phase 2 can be used to encourage people to buy-in to performance measurement. It is designed so that it can be used by a facilitator with multiple teams, each wanting to identify how they can contribute to performance improvement and how their contribution can be measured.

Who is involved

Teams involved in this stage of the process can include:

- Sales teams
- Manufacturing teams (all the people from a single cell)
- Product teams (all the people involved in the design and manufacture of a particular product)
- Functional management teams (all the senior managers from a given function)

- Business process management teams (all the people responsible for managing a particular business process)

What they do

Parts 6 and 7 help teams determine how they can best contribute to the attainment of the top-level business objectives defined in Phase 1.

Parts 8, 9 and 10 repeat Parts 3, 4 and 5 from Phase 1, but this time focusing on performance measures at the level of each team rather than the whole business.

Part 6
What can we use to drive performance towards our objectives?

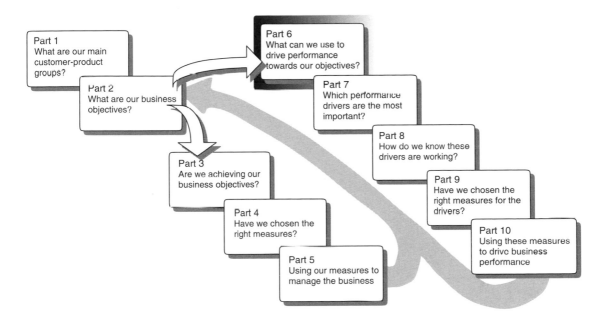

Part 1
What are our main customer-product groups?

Part 2
What are our business objectives?

Part 6
What can we use to drive performance towards our objectives?

Part 7
Which performance drivers are the most important?

Part 3
Are we achieving our business objectives?

Part 8
How do we know these drivers are working?

Part 4
Have we chosen the right measures?

Part 9
Have we chosen the right measures for the drivers?

Part 5
Using our measures to manage the business

Part 10
Using these measures to drive business performance

Aim   *To identify drivers of performance*

Why   To achieve improved business performance in your top-level measures, the initiatives and activities of all members of the organisation will have to be consistent with your business objectives. Part 6 is designed to communicate the business objectives and help the key business teams (Sales, Manufacturing cells, etc.) identify what they can do to support the business objectives and how their progress might be measured.

How   ### Construct a polar fishbone chart framework

Based initially on data collected in Part 2 'What are our business objectives?'.

- To identify what initiatives and activities are being undertaken in the firm

Populate the polar fishbone chart

- Identify and capture performance measures and drivers

The business will already have performance measures. It is important that we capture and build on these rather than ignore them.

Summarise the polar chart

- To make reporting easier

Tips   You can draw up the polar fishbone chart framework before you gather any of the teams together. It is often worth beginning the meeting by explaining where the data shown on the polar fishbone chart have come from and only then asking members of the team to suggest how they can contribute to improved performance.

Objectives				Responsibilities and contributions						Check/ develop measure
Description	Priority	Target		Mnf.	Sales	Dev.	Fin.	H.R.	Qual.	
		Improvement	By when?							
Improve delivery reliability	40	95% delivery on time in full	End of this year	60%	20%		10%		10%	AHR
Ongoing reduction of cost base	40	10%	Year on year	50%	10%	20%	5%	10%	5%	JFM
Reduce customer complaints	20	Reduce current level by 50%	Within 6 months	30%	20%	20%	5%	5%	20%	ADN

Form 5. Customer product group: Precision castings

Constructing a basic polar fishbone chart framework – the facilitator should do this before meeting with each team.

Overriding objective

Take a large sheet of blank paper (flipchart paper is fine). In the middle of the sheet write in large letters 'Long-term business success'.

Business objectives

Around the statement 'Long term business success' write the business objectives that were captured on Form 5 (from Part 2). See 'Tip' below.

Arrows/contribution

Draw large arrows pointing to each business objective. Divide and colour each arrow in proportion to the previously agreed contribution from each business function. These contributions were also recorded on Form 5.

Key

Draw a key to show which colour relates to which function.

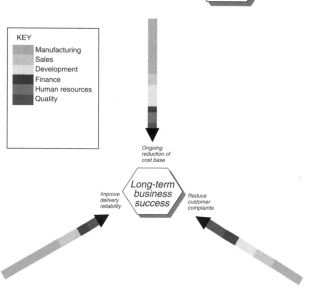

Tip

You will usually find that you have too many objectives to fit on a single polar fishbone chart. To overcome this you need to group your objectives, creating several charts. One way of doing this is to put all the objectives from one dimension of the balanced scorecard together, e.g. all the financial objectives, or all the customer objectives.

Aim *To populate the polar fishbone chart*

How Prior to the session, construct the basic polar fishbone chart. At the session you will also need:

- Blu-tak or pins to mount the chart on the wall
- Flipchart pens
- Handwriting pens
- Post-it® notes of three different colours

Populating the chart is relatively simple:

- Gather all the members of one of the key business teams together (e.g. Sales team, Manufacturing cell)
- Explain how the chart has been constructed
- Ask the team to brainstorm ideas on how it can support the business objectives from its functional perspective
- Record suggestions on activity Post-its® – i.e. Post-its® of one colour
- As each activity is suggested stick it on the polar fishbone chart. See the next page for where to stick the Post-its®.
- Once you have done this, ask the team how the impact of the activity might be measured
- Record their suggestions on measurement Post-its® – i.e. Post-its® of a second colour – and stick them next to the appropriate activity Post-it®
- Repeat the procedure by asking the team to suggest another activity

Repeat this procedure until the team runs out of suggestions. Then explain that you will summarise the polar fishbone chart and when you next meet you will ask the team to split the activities into two categories – must-do and nice-to-do.

Tips To avoid confusion you should always start with a blank polar fishbone chart (i.e. one with no Post-its® on it) whenever taking a new business team through the process.

One of the roles of the facilitator is to watch for suggestions made by different teams which overlap. You need to highlight these and ensure all teams are aware of them.

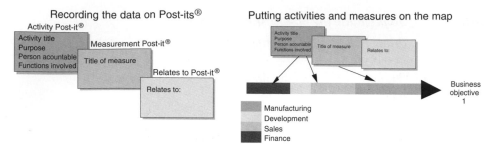

Recording the data on Post-its®

Putting activities and measures on the map

How

Where to stick the Post-it® notes

To decide where to put an activity Post-it®, you should:

- Ask which of the business objectives this activity will have most directly impact

- Stick the activity Post-it® next to the appropriate arrow on the polar fishbone chart

- Ask which functions are involved with this activity

- Draw lines linking the activity to all of the relevant functions

- Ask how the impact of this activity might be measured

- Record the suggestions on a measurement Post-it® and stick it next to the activity Post-it®

- Ask if this activity will have an impact on any of the other business objectives

- If the answer is yes, then ask 'Which ones?' Record the information on a Post-it® of a third colour (the relates-to Post-it®) and stick the Post-it® next to the appropriate activity and measurement Post-its®.

Tips

If any of the activity Post-its® cannot be mapped onto any of the business objectives, then either the activity is not appropriate or there is a business objective missing.

Aim   *To summarise the polar fishbone chart*

The polar fishbone chart may contain in excess of 100 activities and performance measures and hence will not be easy to read. For this reason, it needs to be summarised in report form. (See the example on this page).

How   Begin by listing the business objectives, then:

- From the polar fishbone chart, identify which activities relate to which objectives
- List the associated performance measures against the activities

Business objectives/activities	Associated measures
Improve delivery reliability • improve forecasting accuracy • introduce cells • reduce batch sizes • continuous improvement programme	**Delivery performance** • % deviation forecast from actual • missing measure • average batch size • no. of ongoing quality related continuous improvement activities
Ongoing reduction of cost base • rationalise product range • reduce work in progress • reduce batch sizes • introduce cells • develop long-term supplier partnerships • continuous improvement programme	**Total operating costs** • number of live part numbers • value of work in progress (WIP) • average batch size • missing measure • number of ongoing quality related continuous improvement activities
Reduce customer complaints • introduction of new inspection methods • analysis of undeclared quality failures • deselect/put suppliers on conditional approval • continuous improvement programme • introduce cells • missing measure	**Number of customer complaints** • missing measure • missing measure • % suppliers audited and assessed this year • no. of ongoing quality related continuous improvement activities

On completing Part 6, you will have:

- Explained the objectives of your business to your key business teams.
- Enabled the members of these teams to identify what they can do to ensure business performance improves.
- Helped the members of these teams to identify how they might measure their contribution.

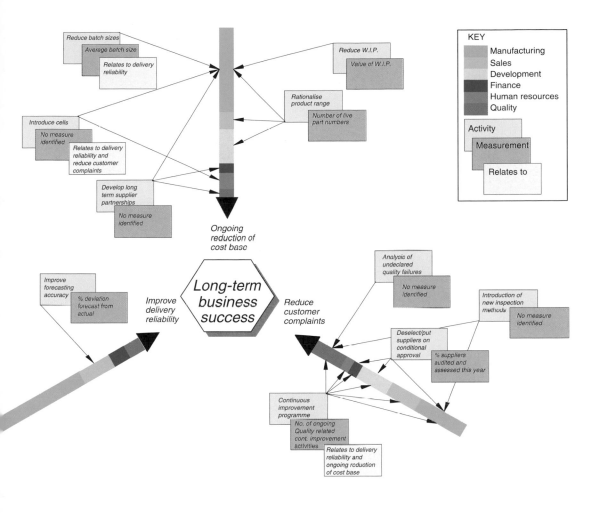

KEY

Manufacturing
Sales
Development
Finance
Human resources
Quality

Activity

Measurement

Relates to

Reduce batch sizes
Average batch size
Relates to delivery reliability

Reduce W.I.P.
Value of W.I.P.

Rationalise product range
Number of live part numbers

Introduce cells
No measure identified
Relates to delivery reliability and reduce customer complaints

Develop long term supplier partnerships
No measure identified

Ongoing reduction of cost base

Improve forecasting accuracy
% deviation forecast from actual

Improve delivery reliability

Long-term business success

Reduce customer complaints

Analysis of undeclared quality failures
No measure identified

Introduction of new inspection methods
No measure identified

Deselect/put suppliers on conditional approval
% suppliers audited and assessed this year

Continuous improvement programme
No. of ongoing Quality related cont. improvement activities
Relates to delivery reliability and ongoing reduction of cost base

Part 7
Which performance drivers are the most important?

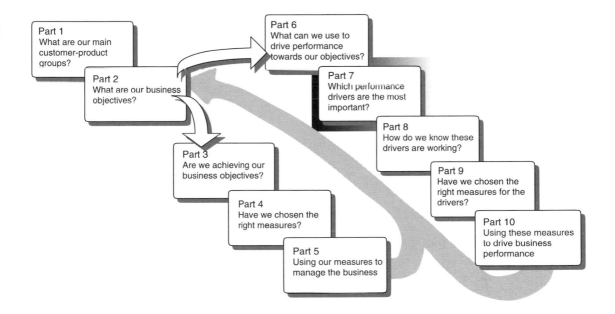

Part 1
What are our main customer-product groups?

Part 2
What are our business objectives?

Part 3
Are we achieving our business objectives?

Part 4
Have we chosen the right measures?

Part 5
Using our measures to manage the business

Part 6
What can we use to drive performance towards our objectives?

Part 7
Which performance drivers are the most important?

Part 8
How do we know these drivers are working?

Part 9
Have we chosen the right measures for the drivers?

Part 10
Using these measures to drive business performance

Aim   *To identify which drivers are key so that appropriate performance measures can be developed*

Why   Each business team that is taken through Part 6 may identify over 100 things that it could do to support the business objectives. Managing such diversity is impractical, so each team needs to decide what it should focus on if it is to maximise the business impact.

How   **Identify key drivers**

- Key drivers are those which will have the greatest impact on whether or not the business objectives are achieved

Evaluate key drivers

- Activities that sometimes appear key can have knock-on effects that are unrecognised. You need to check whether this is the case, and if so, what can be done about it

Agree responsibilities for developing appropriate performance measures

Business objectives/activities	Associated measures
Improve delivery reliability • improve forecasting accuracy • introduce cells • reduce batch sizes • continuous improvement programme	Delivery performance • % deviation forecast from actual • missing measure • average batch size • no. of ongoing quality related continuous improvement activities
Ongoing reduction of cost base • rationalise product range • reduce work in progress • reduce batch sizes • introduce cells • develop long-term supplier partnerships • continuous improvement programme	Total operating costs • number of live part numbers • value of work in progress (WIP) • average batch size • missing measure • number of ongoing quality related continuous improvement activities
Reduce customer complaints • introduction of new inspection methods • analysis of undeclared quality failures • deselect/put suppliers on conditional approval • continuous improvement programme • introduce cells • missing measure	Number of customer complaints • missing measure • missing measure • % suppliers audited and assessed this year • no. of ongoing quality related continuous improvement activities

Aim   *To identify key activities*

How   Gather together all members of the relevant business teams and give them a copy of
            the report summarising their polar fishbone charts (see example below). Then:

- Ask team members individually to classify each activity as either a must-do or a nice-
  to-do.

- Ask them individually to select the 10 most important activities from their must-do
  list. 'Most important' in this context means the activities that will have the greatest
  impact on whether or not the business objectives are achieved.

- Count up the number of times each activity has been identified as a must-do and
  record it on Form 11 as in the example on this page.

- Discuss/debate the resultant list with the entire team until it is reduced to a set that
  the group feels is manageable.

Activity	Number of times identified
Rationalise product range	6
Reduce WIP	6
Develop long-term supplier partnerships	5
Introduce cells	5
Reduce batch sizes	5
Continuous improvement programme	4
Deselect suppliers	4
Analysis of undeclared quality failures	3
Improve forecasting accuracy	2

Form 11. Key drivers

Form 11. Key drivers

Activity	Number of times identified

Use version of Form 11 on the CD.

Aim   *To evaluate key activities*

How   Sometimes activities that appear to be key can have undesirable knock-on effects. The aim of this stage is to check that the activities that appear to be key, really are so.

To do this: Take each activity and business objective in turn and answer the following question:

- Does this activity have:
  ++   a large positive effect on a business objective?
  +   a positive effect on a business objective?
  0   no discernable effect on a business objective?
  –   a negative effect on a business objective?
  ––   a large negative effect on a business objective?

Record your answers on Form 12, on the CD, a blank version is given on the next page.

Having been through this process, ask the group:

- Does everyone agree that these really are the key activities?

- Does anyone wish to add anything else to this list, perhaps something you are not doing now?

Tips   The greatest benefits of doing this are gained through the debate that arises. It is also valuable in that it forces the group to identify explicitly the likely impact of the proposed key activities.

It is vital that this session is allowed to run until consensus has been reached and everyone is comfortable that the key activities have been identified. If necessary reconvene the session once people have had a chance to consider the discussion and gather any data they feel they need.

Activity	Business objectives				Develop measure
	Improve delivery reliability	Reduce customer complaints	Ongoing reduction of cost base		
Rationalise product range	0	0	++		
Reduce WIP	0	0	++		
Develop long-term supplier partnerships	0	0	++		
Introduce cells	+	+	+		
Reduce batch sizes	++	0	++		
Continuous improvement programme	++	++	++		
Deselect suppliers	0	++	0		
Analysis of undeclared quality failures	0	+	0		
Improve forecasting accuracy	++	0	0		

Form 12. Evaluation

Form 12. Evaluation

Activity	Business objectives				Develop measure

Use version of Form 12 on the CD.

Aim   *To agree responsibilities for developing performance measures for each key activity*

How   **Agree responsibilities for developing each performance measure**

A performance measure needs to be developed for each key activity. Each performance measure should be developed by an appropriate, named individual who will report back to the team at a later meeting. The question to be answered for each key activity is:

- Who will be responsible for developing an appropriate measure for this key activity?

Put their initials in the right hand column of Form 12 against the appropriate activity.

Tips   **Appropriate named individuals**

Individuals responsible for developing performance measures should be members of the group that has been defining the key activities.

New measures or old?

For some activities, there may well be performance measures already in use that are perfectly suitable. For others, it may be necessary to create a new measure. In both cases someone who will be responsible for reporting back should be named.

Activity	Business objectives				Develop measure
	Improve delivery reliability	Reduce customer complaints	Ongoing reduction of cost base		
Rationalise product range	O	O	++		AHR
Reduce WIP	O	O	++		JFM
Develop long–term supplier partnerships	O	O	++		KWP
Introduce cells	+	+	+		JFM
Reduce batch sizes	++	O	++		ADN
Continuous improvement programme	++	++	++		AHR
Deselect suppliers	O	++	O		KWP
Analysis of undeclared quality failures	O	+	O		VJD
Improve forecasting accuracy	++	O	O		MJG

Form 12. Evaluation

On completing Part 7, you will have:

- Enabled the members of the teams to identify what they should do to ensure business performance improves.

- Helped the members of the teams to identify how they should measure their contributions.

Part 8
How do we know these drivers are working?

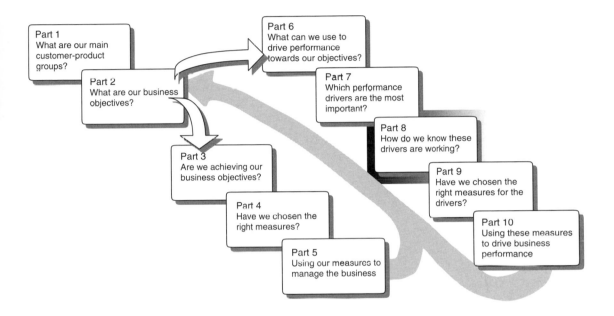

Part 1
What are our main customer-product groups?

Part 2
What are our business objectives?

Part 3
Are we achieving our business objectives?

Part 4
Have we chosen the right measures?

Part 5
Using our measures to manage the business

Part 6
What can we use to drive performance towards our objectives?

Part 7
Which performance drivers are the most important?

Part 8
How do we know these drivers are working?

Part 9
Have we chosen the right measures for the drivers?

Part 10
Using these measures to drive business performance

Catalogue

Aims   *To identify a performance measure for each key driver*

         To complete one performance measure record sheet for each key driver

Why   By the end of Part 7, you will have identified the main performance drivers for your business. The aim of Part 8 is to design performance measures for each of these drivers.

How   Develop a measure for each key driver

The performance measure needs to show:

- How close to (or far from) the target you are.
- How quickly you are moving towards the target.

It also needs to be designed so that it stimulates:

- Appropriate behaviour.
- Managerial action.

The headings on the performance measure record sheet may help in developing the measure. An example of what a completed form might look like, is given on this page; a blank form is given on p. 121 and hints for its completion on p. 120.

Complete performance measure record sheets

     Fill in one performance measure record sheet for each measure. This should help you identify the right measures.

Tips   Work sequentially through the boxes on the performance measure record sheet. Once you have defined the target, the formula should be relatively easy to define.

     Bear in mind that it is the formula that influences the way people behave. Be prepared to loop around the boxes and keep working on the measure until it is practical and will encourage the behaviour you want.

Measure	Product rationalisation
Purpose	Reduce our product range
Relates to	Ongoing reduction of cost base
Target	Reduce live part numbers by 10% by end of year
Formula	$\dfrac{\text{Number of live part numbers now}}{\text{Number of live part numbers at last year end}}$
Frequency	Monthly
Who measures?	F. Jones – Engineering design
Source of data	MRP [materials requirement planning] system
Who acts on the data?	S. Ash – Engineering Director
What do they do?	Establish team to identify further product rationalisation.
Notes and comments	Criteria have to be defined for core products and technologies – i.e. ones that **must** keep.
Date / issue number	21 March 2000 / issue no. 1

Form 6. Performance measure record sheet

Form 6. Performance measure record sheet – guidance notes

Measure	The title of the measure. A good title is self-explanatory, avoids jargon and explains what the measure is and why it is important.
Purpose	If a measure has no purpose then why introduce it? Example purposes: 1. To enable us to monitor the rate of improvement thereby driving down the total cost. 2. To ensure that ultimately all delayed orders are eliminated. 3. To stimulate improvement in our supplier's delivery performance. 4. To ensure that the new product introduction lead time is continually reduced.
Relates to	Identify the business objectives that the measure relates to. As with 'purpose', if the measure being considered does not relate to any business objective then why introduce it?
Target	Targets specify the levels of performance we need to achieve and the timescales within which we need to achieve them. Example targets: 1. X% improvement year on year. 2. Y% reduction during the next 12 months. 3. Achieve Z% delivery performance (on time, in full) by the end of next year.
Formula	How we measure something will affect the way people behave. An appropriately defined formula should drive people towards good business practice. Beware of any formula that might stimulate behaviour we do not want!
Frequency	The frequency with which performance should be recorded and reported is a function of the importance of the measure and the volume of data available.
Who measures?	This box should identify the person who is to collect and report the data.
Source of data	This box should specify where to get the data from. If we want to see how performance changes over time, then we must get our data from the same source each time.
Who acts on the data?	This box should identify the person who is going to act on the data.
What do they do?	Without some action here, the measure is pointless. We may not be able to detail the action to be taken if the performance proves either acceptable or unacceptable as the detail may depend on the context at the time. We can define in general the management process to be followed in the case of acceptable or unacceptable performance. Examples: 1. Set up a continuous improvement group to identify reasons for poor performance and to make recommendations as to how it can be improved. 2. Publish all performance data and an executive summary on the shopfloor as a way of demonstrating commitment to empowerment. 3. Identify commonly occurring problems. 4. Set up a review team, consisting of Sales, Development and Manufacturing personnel to establish whether alternative materials can be used.
Notes and comments	Any specific features, outstanding issues, specific problems, to do with the measure.
Date/issue number	The date and issue number of the record sheet.

Form 6. Performance measure record sheet

Measure	
Purpose	
Relates to	
Target	
Formula	
Frequency	
Who measures?	
Source of data	
Who acts on the data?	
What do they do?	
Notes and comments	
Date/issue number	

Use version of Form 6 on the CD.

The facilitator should test and review each completed performance measure record sheet by asking:

Measure
What should this measure be called?
Does this title explain what the measure is?
Does it explain why the measure is important?
Is it a title that everyone will understand?

Purpose
Why are we introducing this measure?
What do we want it to do?

Relates to

Which of the business objectives does this measure relate to?
Where does it fit on your map of activities and measures?

Target
What level of performance do we desire?
How long will it take us to reach this level of performance?
How does this compare with our competitors?
How good are they currently?
How fast are they improving?

Formula
How are we going to measure this dimension of performance?
Can the formula be defined in mathematical terms?
Is it clear?
Does it explain exactly what data are required?
What behaviour will it induce?
Are there any other behaviours that we want it to induce?
Is the scale we are using appropriate?
How accurate will the data generated be?
Are they accurate enough?
If we use an average, how much data will we lose?
Is this acceptable?
Do we need to know the spread of performance?

Frequency
How often should this measure be made?
How often should it be reported?
Will we be able to collect and analyse the data rapidly enough?
How much delay will there be in improving performance along this dimension?

Who measures?
Who, by name, is actually responsible for making this measure?

Source of data
Where will they get the data from?

Who acts on the data?
Who, by name, is actually responsible for ensuring that performance along this dimension improves?

What do they do?

What actions will they be taking to do this?

Tips

A useful concept is that of the perfectly executed order. When defining measures ask: are you really capturing everything you need to capture? An order can be classified as delivered on time if it arrives at the customer's facility on the day it was promised. Of course this may not be the day the customer originally wanted it. Similarly if the order arrives on time but incomplete, or the invoice overcharges the customer, is it a perfectly executed order?

Once the measure has been defined ask how practical it is. If it is not going to be practical to collect and analyse the data, try to identify a simpler measure. The trick when designing measures is to adopt the simplest measure you can that is consistent with what you are trying to achieve. Very complex measures become expensive to implement and can lead to problems in terms of time lags.

On completing Part 8, you will have:

- Formally documented performance measures for your key drivers.
- Identified who should be responsible for managing performance improvement.
- Defined what they should do if performance does not appear to be improving.

Part 9
Have we chosen the right measures for the key drivers?

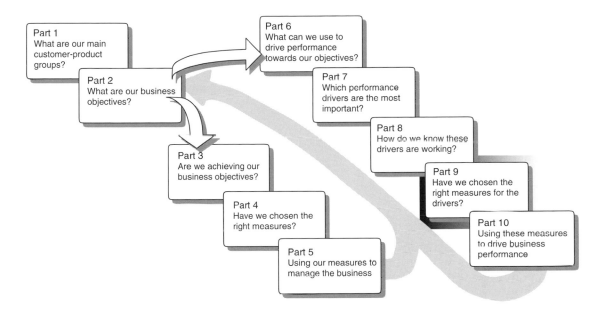

Aims   *To check all members of each business team agree with all the performance measures that their team will use*

To establish a process for tracking progress with the implementation of each measure

To check whether there are any barriers to implementation

Why   It is now time for each business team to take a step back and check if it is happy with its performance measures. This is the last chance it will have before going live with them.

How   Check that everyone agrees with the performance measures for the key drivers. It is likely that each performance measure will have been seen by relatively few people so far. At this stage the rest of the business team needs to be given the opportunity to comment.

Check whether there are any barriers to implementation. Are your reward systems consistent with your performance measures? If not, do you need to change your reward systems?

Are there any existing performance measures inconsistent with your new measures? If so, should you delete some of your existing measures?

Tips   By the end of this part you should have a formally agreed, balanced set of key driver performance measures. Once Part 9 has been completed the record sheets should be written up neatly and subject to formal change procedures – i.e. once the measures have been agreed at this meeting they should not be changed without formal notification.

Note: You should repeat this part with every business team that has been through Parts 6, 7 and 8. Each team should consider only its own measures.

Aim   *To check all members of a team agree with the measures their team will use*

How   Use Form 7 shown on this page. A version is available on the CD and a larger blank form is shown on the next page.

1. Arrange a meeting involving everybody in the business team.

2. Invite each person to give a brief presentation explaining the performance measure(s) they have developed.

3. Encourage the audience to pull each measure to pieces and identify whether it is likely to lead to any undesirable behaviours. Useful tests at this stage include:

• *Truth* – Is it definitely measuring what it is meant to?

• *Focus* – Is the measure measuring only what it is meant to?

• *Consistency* – Is the measure consistent whenever it is measured and whoever measures?

• *Clarity* – Are the results open to ambiguous interpretation?

• *Access* – Can the data be readily communicated and easily understood?

• *'So what?'* – Can, and will, the measure be acted upon?

• *Cost* – How expensive is it to collect, collate and analyse the data?

• *Timeliness* – Can the data be collected and analysed quickly enough?

• *Gaming* – Will the measure encourage undesirable behaviours?

4. After each performance measure has been presented check that everybody agrees with the target as defined on the performance measure record sheet.

5. Nominate someone (a single person) to own the measure. This person (the owner), will be expected in the future to:

• Keep track of progress on this particular dimension of performance.

• Propose corrective action plans as and when they are needed.

Tips   When asking people to prepare their presentations limit them to one slide only – the performance measure record sheet.

It is worth trying to make all the necessary modifications at the meeting, although often it will prove necessary to repeat the measures review process, especially for those measures designed to track dimensions of performance that are complex.

Performance measure	Who will present	Modification required	Target agreed	Owner approved

Form 7. Sign off

Form 7. Sign off

Performance measure	Who will present	Modification required	Target agreed	Owner approved

Use version of Form 7 on the CD.

Aim   *To establish a process for tracking progress with the implementation of each measure*

How   Implementation of measures requires the completion of four distinct activities. First the measure must be designed. Then it must be reviewed and accepted. Next the necessary data collection processes have to be established. Finally the measure can be used to manage performance. By this stage of the process all of the measures should have been designed, and a significant number of them will have been accepted, although there may be others that require further work. Use form 8 to capture progress to date with each measure and agree a process for reviewing progress in the future.

Tips   While designing measures is intellectually challenging, implementation is often the point at which most measurement initiatives fail. There are numerous reasons for this, but the most significant is that the time and effort required to establish the necessary data capture and collation infrastructure becomes too great.

It is therefore really important to plan at the implementation stage an appropriate review process so that the business team regularly review progress of the implementation effort.

Measure	Owner	Measure designed? (Y/N)	Measure agreed? (Y/N)	Data available? (Y/N)	Measure used (Y/N)
Delivery reliability	AHR	Y	N	Y	N
Cost base	JFN	N	N	N	N
Customer complaints	ADN	N	N	N	N

Form 8. Measure implementation

Form 8. Measure implementation

Measure	Owner	Measure designed? (Y/N)	Measure agreed? (Y/N)	Data available? (Y/N)	Measure used (Y/N)

Use version of Form 8 on the CD.

Aim   *To check if there are any other barriers to implementation*

How   Give each member of the group between six and ten Post-it® notes and ask them:

- To identify, and write down on the Post-it® notes, the three to five things that they think will most hinder the successful introduction of the performance measures (one per Post-it®).

- To identify, and write down on the Post-it® notes, the three to five things that they think will most help the successful introduction of the performance measures (one per Post-it®).

Now invite each member of the group to stick their Post-its® on to Form 9 as shown in the example on this page.
    A blank version is shown on the next page.

Then:

- Extract the main barriers to implementation and identify what can be done about them.

- List the factors that will make implementation easier and decide how their impact can be maximised.

Tips   Typical barriers include factors such as: lack of resource, the fact that the organisation's reward systems are inconsistent with the performance measures being proposed, the concern that people may feel threatened by the performance measures.
    Factors that make implementation easier include: the possibility of publishing the measures on notice boards or in a newsletter, the existence of a forum where the performance can be reviewed, the opportunity to link the implementation to an existing initiative, a total quality management programme.

	Factors that will make implementation easier	Proposed measures	Factors that will make implementation difficult
Factors that will affect all measures	Publication of results in newsletter		Existing sales incentive scheme
			Fear that the measures will be used as a stick
			Emphasis on machine utilisation
Factors that will affect specific measures		Delivery performance	
		Cost base	
	The link to customer satisfaction programme	Customer complaints	

Form 9. Barriers

Form 9. Barriers

	Factors that will make implementation easier	Proposed measures	Factors that will make implementation difficult
Factors that will affect all measures			
Factors that will affect specific measures			

Use version of Form 9 on the CD.

On completing Part 9, you will have:

- Established that each business team agrees with the performance measures that their team will use.

- Established an appropriate process for regularly reviewing progress with the implementation of the measures.

- Established whether there are any barriers to implementation, and if so, what can be done about them.

Part 10
Using these measures to drive business performance

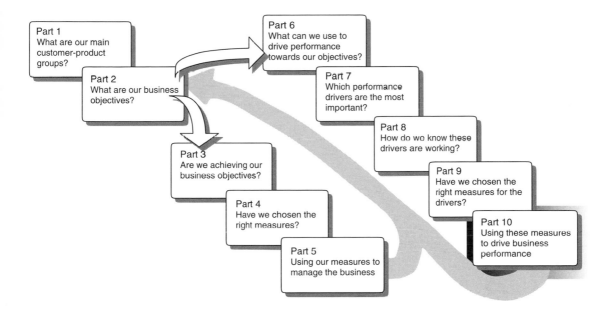

Part 1
What are our main customer-product groups?

Part 2
What are our business objectives?

Part 3
Are we achieving our business objectives?

Part 4
Have we chosen the right measures?

Part 5
Using our measures to manage the business

Part 6
What can we use to drive performance towards our objectives?

Part 7
Which performance drivers are the most important?

Part 8
How do we know these drivers are working?

Part 9
Have we chosen the right measures for the drivers?

Part 10
Using these measures to drive business performance

Aims	*To agree an agenda for future performance reviews*
	To agree a mechanism for reviewing the performance measurement system
	To conduct successful performance reviews

Why   Performance measures are simply a means to an end. All the time and effort you have spent identifying and defining your measures will be wasted unless you establish a review mechanism which ensures that action follows measurement.

How   Agree an agenda for future performance reviews

Having finished the formal development of your performance measurement system you now need to agree how you will use the performance measures on an ongoing basis.

To do this you need to address the following questions:

- How will performance be reviewed?
- How frequently will it be reviewed?
- In what forum will it be reviewed?
- Who will be responsible for organising the reviews?
- Who will be involved?
- What will be the agenda?
- When will the first one take place?

Agree a mechanism for reviewing the performance measurement system

Performance measurement systems are not static. Rather they evolve as market conditions change and performance improves. Too often new performance measures are introduced, without old ones being deleted.

To avoid this, you need to agree a mechanism that will help you maintain your measurement system on an ongoing basis.

Conduct successful performance reviews

- What makes performance reviews successful in practice?
- What is the role of the chairman?
- What is the role of the facilitator?

Tips   You are likely to find that it will take a couple of review meetings before the group falls into the habit of discussing action plans rather than simply reviewing last month's performance.

One of the jobs of the facilitator is to help the group make this transition. A simple way of doing this is to keep asking: 'What do you think we should do to help improve performance?'.

Aim   *To agree an agenda for future performance reviews*

How   Performance measures are only valuable when they stimulate appropriate action. Performance reviews should be structured so that they ensure this happens.

Questions you need to answer at this stage include:

- How will performance be reviewed?

    The key to a good performance review is to have a mechanism that not only enables you to assess how well you have performed, but that also stimulates the production of appropriate corrective action plans. Many firms have found the mechanism developed by Ford Electronics a useful way of doing this. See example right and on the following pages.

- How frequently will performance be reviewed and in what forum?

    Performance measures should be reviewed on a monthly basis. It is recommended that you do not set up a new management meeting to review performance. Instead the performance reviews should become an integral part of an activity that is already ongoing e.g. the board meeting.

- Who will be responsible for organising the reviews?

    The owner of each measure should be responsible for collating the data they need and for presenting them at the review. It is often useful to nominate an overall co-ordinator whose role is to keep the necessary records and take the minutes of the meeting.

- Who will be involved?

    This will be company specific. At the very least, however, the owners of all the performance measures will have to be present.

- What will be on the agenda?

    Typically, the agenda for the review will contain the following items: a review of previous minutes, a review of the key performance measures, agreed action plans and any other business.

- When will the first review take place?

    Why not fix a date for the first review meeting now?

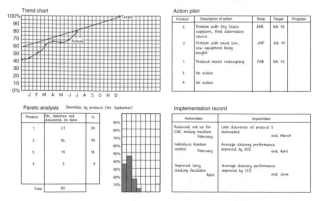

Form 10. Ford visualisation

Form 10. The Ford visualisation

On the next page, there is the blank form of this chart for photocopying. Alongside is a brief description of what data should go into each part of the chart and below is an example filled in with data from earlier examples in this workbook.

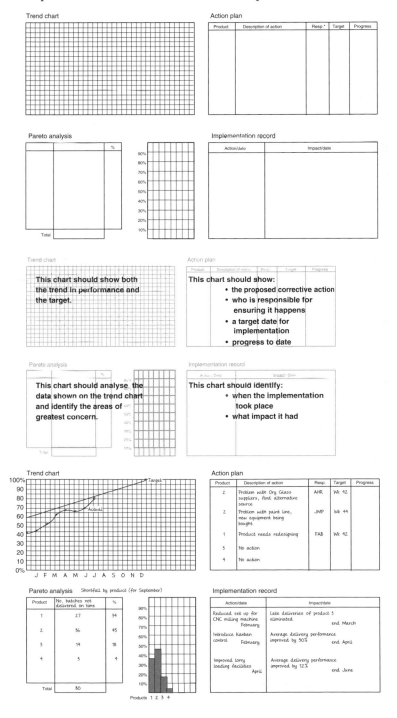

Form 10. The Ford visualisation

Trend chart

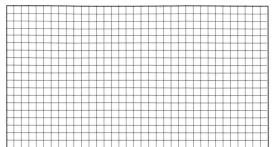

Action plan

Product	Description of action	Resp.*	Target	Progress

Pareto analysis

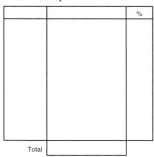

		%
Total		

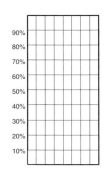

90%
80%
70%
60%
50%
40%
30%
20%
10%

Implementation record

Action/date	Impact/date

Aim   *To agree a mechanism for reviewing the performance measurement system*

How   Performance measurement systems are often allowed to expand to the extent that they become unmanageable. So before going live with your performance measurement system, address the following questions:

- Do we have any mechanisms in place to which we could tie a review of the performance measurement system?

- Who will be responsible for ensuring the review takes place?

- How will they go about it?

Tips   Often the review of the performance measurement system is tied to the annual budget cycle. Other options include linking it to the strategic planning cycle or the production of the annual accounts.

Aim   *To conduct successful performance reviews*

How   Always review the last set of minutes.

Review all the key driver performance measures.

Agree actions.

Tips   Get the measures printed on overhead transparencies and projected onto a screen at the review meeting. This focuses everyone's attention on the measure under discussion. Experience has shown that reviewing measures in a reporting pack (where everyone has their own copy) is not as effective as viewing a measure projected on a screen.

Do not be surprised if the first review does not work as well as you had hoped. What tends to happen is that the group's understanding of the review process evolves over time. Initially people tend to use the review as a forum for reporting how well they are doing. Later they begin to understand that what is really required is action plans to improve performance.

To ensure that this group learning takes place it is vital that the chairman and the facilitator continually ask the owner of each measure:

- Are we on course to achieve the target?

- If not, what do you propose we do?

If you decide to publish the measures it is also worth considering copying them onto different coloured pieces of paper. January can be the yellow month, February the red month, etc. This provides a visual signal that the data on your notice boards has changed and is up to date.

It is also worth publishing a notice specifying who owns each measure. This is a useful way of signalling senior management commitment and making explicit who is responsible for each dimension of performance.

Upon completing Part 10, you will have:

- Agreed an agenda for future performance reviews.
- Held a couple of performance review meetings to iron out any teething problems.
- Confidence that the measures you have chosen really can be used to drive improvements in business performance.

The Strategy and Performance CD

Mac

- Insert the CD in your drive.
- The Mac_Readme file will open automatically and explain how to use the CD.

PC Win 95, 98, NT

- Insert the CD in your drive. The Windows installer will automatically run to take you through the installation process. (Note: There is a README.txt file on the CD with more detailed information.)

To use the blank PDF versions of forms on the CD

- Insert the CD in your drive.
- Cancel the auto-installation process.
- Right-click on your CD drive icon and select 'Explore' from the menu.
- Open the folder 'Pdf forms' and double-click on the file 'FormsIndex.pdf'.

  (Alternatively, copy the folder 'Pdf forms' onto your hard drive first.)

Coventry University